IBOS OF NIGERIA
AND THEIR CULTURAL WAYS

IBOS OF NIGERIA
AND THEIR CULTURAL WAYS

Aspects of Behavior,

Attitudes, Customs,

Language and Social Life

COLUMBUS OKOROIKE

iUniverse, Inc.
New York   Bloomington

IBOS OF NIGERIA AND THEIR CULTURAL WAYS
Aspects of Behavior, Attitudes, Customs, Language and Social Life

Copyright © 2009 by Columbus Okoroike

iUniverse books may be ordered through booksellers or by contacting:

iUniverse
1663 Liberty Drive
Bloomington, IN 47403
www.iuniverse.com
1-800-Authors (1-800-288-4677)

ISBN: 978-0-595-52073-2 (pbk)
ISBN: 978-0-595-62140-8 (ebk)

Printed in the United States of America

iUniverse rev. date: 01/08/09

Contents

Ibo people of Nigeria are not known outside of the country of Nigeria. The study of the Ibos and their Igbo language has been neglected by the European and western alike. Little has been written about the culture and art of this spiritual and religious yet symbolic people of Africa. They are a dynamic people but have been hurt tremendously by cultural evolution during the last fifty years or so. Their origin is not well documented but records found here and there point to the fact that Igbo people migrated from the middle belt and ended up mostly on the eastern banks of the River Niger in Nigeria before expanding to other areas. The central Igbo land is the present day Imo and Abia state areas, and form the central core Igbo language, with major differences in dialect.

Although the Portuguese were the first European to make contact with the Ibos before the British could make in-roads from the coast, it was the British that were able to convince of the desirability or attractiveness of their imperialistic ideology on the people. To the detriment of the Igbo people, language and culture, the British prevailed over the Portuguese with more sophisticated weaponry, and in 1914, amalgamated the territories into protectorate states of Nigeria. They did not see the problem of cultural incompatibility, or they just plainly discounted it. The difference in language, which some would call tribes, culture, religion and geography will always manifest itself in the governance and unity or the lack thereof in this multi-ethnic nation.

To be interested in Igbo people of Nigeria, you may want to know their culture traits, habits and social life. It may not be necessary to learn their language, since the Ibos are English-speaking by virtue of the British colonization of almost all of West Africa. Ibos are by no means different than people from other cultures in terms of their preferences in music, literature and art of the people, their culture has been defined by their uniqueness, talent, creativity and resourcefulness through the centuries. Igbo art and democracy preceded civilization, as the Europeans came to realize in their recent anthropological finds; at Uturu Okigwe, and Igbo-Ukwu Village, of Igbo land.

How the Ibos interact, clothing, religious influence, deviation from known and acceptable western culture and such effects socially and behaviorally, may have been generalized a million times over especially, in the areas of marriage, relationships, infant baptism, polygamy and concubinage. Some may hold true, others may not. Hopefully, this will educate, enlighten and create an understanding of the Igbo people of Southeastern Nigeria and their culture. A lot of people who want to know where I am from, are mostly interested in my culture. They may have already known about Nigeria, but why Ibos are or what makes them different from the other ethnic groups and what it is that influenced us differently, may not be all common knowledge.

INTRODUCTION

The mystic of language differences is difficult to explain, except that we all are aware that different people speak different languages and uphold different value systems, behave in certain ways and are culturally different from others. Culture traits and habits of one people may be different but should not be judged as better or worse. Mystic because this may have originated from biblical tower of Babel, the construction of which was halted as was held in the book of Genesis due to confusion of tongues, different voices and sudden differences in language resulting in lack of communication and comprehension. Here, an attempt is made to try to explain culture from the dictionary definition which is the customary beliefs social forms and material traits of a racial or social group; the set of shared attitudes, values, and practices that characterizes a people.

Culture will also be defined and interpreted here in terms of music, dance, literature and art of a people. It consists of what the Ibo has accumulated and passed on down the generations. People are proud to tell others of their culture, because it is who they are and what makes them unique. I am proud to talk about Igbo culture, some of which are common knowledge to Igbo speaking people many others may have been read in books or perceived from mere proximity to a

3

few Nigerian occasions here in the United States and abroad. Culture contains elements that model people's daily lives and in the case of Igbo speaking people of Nigeria, this may play an important role in waking up the cultural intellect of this unique and proud nation.

The aim of this book is also to create awareness and a more comfortable feeling toward Igbo speaking people and their culture and hopefully leading to foreigners broadening their knowledge of this part of Nigeria and Africa in general. To demonstrate my intense feeling that to understand something, you have to draw it, and because my drawings will not look better than pictures I find in my research, I have included photos from different sources and thank them for their permission, explicit or implied. American hungers to know about the Igbo people of Nigeria.

Ibos are everywhere on this planet earth, but unfortunately little is known about the Igbo language outside of Nigeria. Yet they are described as one of the most dynamic tribes in all of Africa. The evolutionary process of the culture toward westernization could be one culprit. This westernization process became a trend that grossly disregarded the cultural sensitivities of the Igbo human life, language, thinking characteristics and concepts. Igbo culture is uniquely Ibo, evidenced in their manner of dressing, the language they speak, what they eat, the way they eat, dance, trade, worship or organize themselves both in public and in private. Igbo children born outside the land are deficient in every aspect of the Igbo ways. We must teach them their cultural heritage so that they will be proud of where they come from, and to understand why they must not let the Igbo language die.

Documentation of Igbo life and culture is fragmented but they are geographically found in South-eastern Nigeria and have dispersed to some area in the middle belt bordering Enugu. The central Igbo land is around Owerri and all other states that help form the core of Igbo tribe prior to further migration. Topics covered here range from religious and spiritual issues to social-cultural and language issues. Hopefully, this is about the culture and language of the Ibos, aimed at educating our non-Ibos children of a very important people, who are in danger of losing their language, art, culture, identity through evolution and westernization.

Ibos speak Igbo language and use expressions and proverbs to give words appropriate and deeper meanings. In Igbo a single word may have numerous meanings, and in majority of situations, do not have literary translations. Ideas are also communicated by using a combination of Igbo and English language translations. This is a deliberate attempt to teach and explain to the reader a few Igbo words and phrases so as to have fun with it, as well as get educated.

CHAPTER ONE

ABBREVIATIONS AND ACRONYMS

There are no abbreviations in standard written Igbo language usage. Abbreviations are only found and used in names of individuals or things and are capitalized, for example:

Chi Chineke (God the creator)

Ik Ikechukwu (God's power)

Abbreviation of proper nouns could be the person's initials, and are capitalized, for instance:

C.O (Columbus Okoroike)

J.C. (Joseph)

J.K (Jacob)

D (Darling)

D (daddy)

Mr. (Mister)

Dr. (Doctor)

Some abbreviations are short written form of a word, for example:

Hon. (Honorable)

Prez (President)

Pa (Papa)

Ma (Mama)

Ma'am (madam)

There are however, few abbreviations in this book just because they will be helpful to the reader.

ACRONYMS

Acronym is a word formed from the initial letter or letters of each of the successive parts or major parts of a compound term. An acronym is also any word formed from the initial letters of the words of a descriptive phrase or a proper noun and is usually written in capital letters, for example:

OPEC - Organization of Petroleum Exporting Countries

UN - United Nations

NCC - National Council of Churches

G.C.E - General Certificate of Education

Most written Igbo mimic the English language but rules of the diction differ enormously. There are however, no acronyms in Igbo language, or are not used in widely read written language prose

CHAPTER TWO

GREETINGS TO MY PEOPLE

Ndi be anyi nde ewo! Unu a buo la chi? Ekele diri unu.

Ndi be anyi kwenu! Igbo kwenu!! Ndi be anyi mma mma nu!!!

Unu a nwuchula anwuchu! Umu nnam biri kwa nu!!

Egbe bere ugo bere nke si ibe ya eberele, nku kwaa ya!

Ndi eze ekele diri unu

Ndi Nze na Ozo, ekele m unu

Oha na Eze ekele m unu

Ndi Igbo kwenu, Igbo kwenu, kwezuo nu

GREETINGS

There are several ways the Ibos salute people at meetings. Most people express good wishes in the English way, although the sound is quite different to the foreigner.

Unu abuola chi	good morning
Unu aputala ura	good morning
Ehihe oma	good afternoon
Kedu ka unu di	how are you - plural
Mma mma nu	You are looking good - plural
Unu anuo la	How are you – plural
Ana m ekele unu	I salute you
Ekele diri unu	greetings to you – plural
Ndi be anyi unu anuo la	How are you, my people
Ka chi buo	Good night
Ka chi fuo "	
Buo nu chi "	
Ka oduwa ubochi ozo	Till next time

The above are phrases that serve as salutations at meetings. People use them to greet each other while passing or as they shake hands before starting a conversation. If you want to acknowledge others without stopping, you may say:

> Ka emesia
> A ga na ahu
> A ga ahukorita
> We shall see
> We shall meet again

If someone meets you while you are eating or about to eat, at social event, crowded gathering, festivals, and much more elaborate circles, such bodies are greeted thus:

> Igbo Kwenu
> Igbo Kwenu!
> Okigwe Knenu!
> Kwezuenu!

Each of the greetings is responded with a resounding Yaa!

These are a few celebrated greetings in Igbo custom in the plural. This would apply at gatherings, festive occasions, when to address an audience, at meetings or concert halls. These are not the typical way one would greet a parent, a senior, elderly person or subordinates, but age groups, yes. These are greetings that get people to focus their attention to you and what you have to say.

Greetings to you my people, people of the world and especially you who now have this book in your hand. The Ibos are very customary, traditional and respectful. It is therefore important to start this book with an introductory greeting, typical and traditional of an Igbo speaker about to address his audience. As you commence reading this book picture yourself standing at my front door, and you press the doorbell, as you wait to be welcomed into my residence. I am as typical as an Ibo as you can imagine, with hope you are imagining the good qualities. Unlike most European writers who get most of their information from people they meet and interview in hotel lobbies, my writing is based on knowledge, experience, research, first rate information and interview of traditional and cultural leaders at festivals and ceremonies. I asked questions about the initiation ceremonies I participated in growing up in Okai village, Umuna in Okigwe, some of which were privileged and too expensive for other young adults to participate. Also, my observations at Igbo gatherings, parties, ceremonies, private homes, and discussions and interactions with people of diverse disciplines convinced me that writing a book will be better than just publishing an article or two on the internet website of any related magazine out there.

The writing of this book was delayed momentarily, but after prolonged hesitation hardly attributable to inability to reach a firm decision, the justification cropped up from arguments at several social and cultural events I attended in the Northern California area. Besides, most American friends and colleagues know and ask about Kenya, Ghana, South Africa, Somalia, Ethiopia, Liberia and even Uganda than Nigeria. In college a few ladies approached me on regular basis and ask me to speak Swahili, and teach them how to say certain words in Swahili. There is frequent news about crude oil supply disruption in Nigeria, and corruption, and Obasanjo wanting to amend the Nigerian constitution so he could remain president for three consecutive terms or more, but nothing more on a positive note.

News about a major talk show host in the United States of America, adopting a few towns in Somalia and South Africa in the year, 2005. When further news of that personality spending and investing millions of dollars of their private money to improve the lots of quite a few people in many parts of Africa through some Angel Network, I wondered if any of these millionaires has heard of the plight of Ibos and if so, would ever plan to visit the Igbo land. A recently established Leadership Academy for girls in South Africa so far is a huge success and undertaking by any stretch of the imagination. I am sure many in the West have forgotten if they heard of the plight of the Ibos and the civil war that devastated the Ibos from 1966 to 1970 and to wonder what has become of the people today. Events around the world today remind me what I and the people in Southeastern Nigeria experienced during the Nigeria/Biafra civil war of 1966 to 1970.

As recently as 2006, millionaire movie stars were into adopting the country of Namibia, establishing residence there and even delivering their babies in that part of Africa in June of 2006. Soon after that, popular singer, Brittany Spears made a huge announcement about wanting to also deliver her second pregnancy in Namibia, and if possible move to and establish domicile in the country. That was before her constant runs with media photographers and her fight for the custody of her two children. I would love to hear that any of these mega personalities is interested in exploring Okigwe in Imo State of Nigeria or the Ibos. May be they can contact me to lead them

Here are some aspects of Igbo culture, people, language, attitudes to strangers and ways of life that could prepare you or one for going, meeting and doing business with the people. Three of my four little children wonder aloud about life in my birthplace, Nigeria. This was after they have watched the food my wife and I eat, the way we eat, the different language we speak when we called Nigeria over the telephone, and more importantly, the type of questions their teachers asked them about their parents, their legal status and educational attainments. My daughter was the first to try the variations of Nigerian dishes she envied us eat, but complained vigorously about the hot pepper with which we spiced our food. At certain times of the year, projects about family tree were assigned to my children, though not all at one time. My children will engage us all over again, especially me the father just because I am always around, and I never sleep in the afternoon, or go to bed before them. My work schedule is such that I leave the house thirty minutes before they go to school, and I always made it home less than an hour after they have arrived. Well, this is not about me except that my parenting instinct has always been very strong.

The United States of America is a country of immigrants, made up of people who come to this country to take up permanent residence. Many of these immigrants naturalize thereby owing allegiance to the government and are entitled to protection and privileges that result from naturalization. When children are born, they arrive without the appropriate knowledge of the history of their family tree. They grow in this culture only to be informed or realize by observation their unique situation. Although this may not be a bad situation, and in majority of instances, the new found home offers much more opportunities and better means of livelihood that would have been the case if raised like their parents in the countries they migrated from. Abandoning our culture all together is like stripping ourselves and our children of our identity, language and the essence of creation. My wife and I now acknowledge the fact that mistakes were made not to have taught our children the Igbo language when they were learning to speak. My wife discouraged it then, as some mothers think they know what is best for their children because suddenly they consider themselves authorities on the subject. Her only reason was that teaching our children Igbo language in an English speaking country would confuse and rob them the opportunity of mastering English language. If I tried a dozen times to persuade my wife that children can learn ten different languages effectively at quite an early age without being confused, she vehemently opposed it a thousand times over. Now, our children feel cheated that they are unable to fluently speak their parents' language.

As they grew up they from time to time ask me; dad, how do you say thank you in Igbo? What are you and mom saying? Are you talking about us? When are you going to teach us to speak Igbo like you? How do you say "good night, good morning, good afternoon, and get the heck out of here in your language? How do you say "I am thirsty in

Igbo language? And the questioning continues until I made effort to move on to something else. They want to speak the language of their parents which is good for them and the Ibo heritage and posterity. Sometimes it becomes difficult to explain the sounds of words because they mispronounce almost all the Igbo words even on their best days on their best efforts.

There is a danger that the future generation of Ibos will miss out on the Igbo culture, identity and social life because they are born in foreign cultures that are different from the one culture that makes them unique individuals. We must therefore make efforts to start early to overcome our over excitement and eagerness to call ourselves Americans that we lose sight of what we are doing to the future generation of Americans who also must know and appreciate where their parents migrated from. The language and cultural problem is uniquely the problem of Ibos everywhere and it is high time we did something serious to address the issue.

This book is not about me nor is it about the situation in my household. It is about a culture that must not be forgotten, a proud heritage that will remain the essence of human origin which is the Ibo breed, the human stock and class kind that is recognized as a cut above all, anywhere and in any endeavor. If we lose our Igbo system of communicating ideas or feelings by our use of conventionalized Igbo signs, sounds, gestures or tone-marks, we lose our meaning. Most of Igbo admissible expressions, vocabulary and phraseology have no close substitutes. What we do sometimes is complete our Igbo sentences with one or two English words or expression. The colonial ambassadors to Nigeria, and more especially those who infiltrated Igbo land accomplished their goal of establishing British colony, but their subversion and propaganda furthered their cause and injured the Igbo institution and damaged the Ibo person. One instance was the introduction of religion in place of our ancestral ways of worship, and another is the Language. We abandoned "Ofor Na Ogu" and accepted Communion and the Blessed Eucharist.

We were made to believe that the reverend fathers also called priests were holy and celibate. Now we are hearing things different, the spiritual communion with God turned out to be through the filthy fingers of the not-so-holier-than thou priests. When I read about what were uncovered about the past of priests in Boston Archdiocese and those in New Mexico in the United States, I cried a million tears for the people of Africa and especially the Ibos where Catholic religion is predominant. That part of Africa was flooded with Irish priests who only conducted church services in Latin language. They were like bulls in a china shop. They feared no human, took what they wanted, killed who they wanted, bulldozed through the youths and the villages with no iota of challenges. Ibos thought that priests were doing the work of God, and were holy persons.

In the United States where fewer states were Catholics, priests are now being defrocked, and banned from exercising functions of priesthood, or removed from positions of honor or privilege. Many have been jailed and even one priest was reported of having died in prison recently. In Igbo land, no major press or the television station has reported or shown a clip of the incidents uncovered in the United States in regard. I am sure Catholic priests performed worse acts and preyed on young boys and girls in Igbo land, especially in Onitsha, Enugu, Aba, Afikpo, Orlu, Okigwe, Owerri, Umuahia, Ihiala, PortHarcourt and numerous other towns. They erected their mighty cathedrals to show for looting the local economy, built a few mission schools and took advantage of the unsuspecting youth.

In Igbo land, priests were never to do any wrong, they were listened to religiously, as they dictated what was right and what was wrong in Igbo tradition and culture. They were given food, livestock, lands, labor, housing, the pulpit and precious time left from the time they took from the Igbo community. Their word was gospel, to put it mildly, if not the word of God. They came from all parts of Europe with nothing but their Bible, penetrated the most interior of Southeastern Nigeria and succeeded in persuading against every Igbo cultural observance and traditional way.

In return, Ibos were promised Heaven, that on our final day, we do not just die, that our soul would go to heaven and rejoice forever, unless we died with sin, and those would be the ones that would go to hell and say hello to the devil, in an eternal fire.

Religion is nothing if it is not an essential part of culture, what makes aspect of religion so emotionally contentious is that they are eminently cultural, whatever other elements society and managers of religious organizations attribute to them. (Uchendu: 1965).

CHAPTER THREE

UNTRUTHS AND GENERALIZATIONS

There have been for years, numerous untruths and generalizations about the African continent in general. There equally has been also a general lack of knowledge of the Igbo of South Eastern Nigeria, and their culture. Here is an effort to at least stir up interest and to offer an insight as to how a foreigner can interact with the people from Nigeria and especially the Igbo people of Nigeria. It may be necessary for foreigners to learn the Igbo language and culture, and if possible, observe Ibos in a cultural activity to really understand the Ibo man.

The Igbo culture is underrepresented in scholarly books and virtually unknown to the outside world, even to the future generations of this ethnic Nigerians including my four children who were all born in California, United States of America. The good news is that while the above are all true and speak volumes, the Ibos speak English language as if it is their mother tongue and are willing to speak and at the same time interpret to the non Igbo and the non-Igbo speaking.

When the Europeans made their way into West Africa as early as the 16th century, they infested the riverine communities and left indelible marks. Priceless and precious art objects and material wealth were taken by force and shipped to Britain, France and even Spain. The Ibos, a little in the hinterland in the Eastern Region of Nigeria escaped the ravage as well as the missionary invasion and survived the rampage. The Igbo art and culture thus thrived because being in the hinterland, and blessed with natural boundaries and the strong belief in their protection by very powerful ancestors, the Europeans had more difficulty reaching them, compared to their ease of accessibility to the Yoruba or Benin areas.

The Igbo culture is very broad in scope, and depending on whose definition one chooses to feel comfortable with, multifaceted. This is evident in villages, though only a few miles apart exhibit striking societal differences in traditions. These traditions and societal differences resonate in the dialects, which are quite numerous by any stretch of imagination. The little rivers, streams and even the seasonal rivulets that dissect the Igbo land contribute in large measures in the differences mentioned above, as they trickle through the towns and villages, in their destined task of natural resource allocation.

There are also differences in the modes of livelihood and subsistence among the Igbos. Those who live near the open-air major market towns are slightly culturally different, when compared to the villagers who live a few miles away from the rural markets. The former are more likely to engage in petty trading small scale trading while the later tend to spend more time in their farms and gardens in genuine efforts at making a living, the old fashioned crude farming way.

The culture of the Ibo people of Nigeria will very much be appreciated if studied in the light of that which makes the people alike, rather than where they differ. The Igbo culture is of greatest interest to people from other cultures because, of all the information requested of me when approached, patterns of behavior, habits and marriage have been the most traits people are curious and very eager to know about. Their self-reliance, pride, strength, and undying desire for economic and social order as deeply rooted in unique cultural heritage will light up interest in the study of Igbo cultural ways.

Art is another element of the Igbo culture that makes for interesting study. Art molds this unique people's behavior in their daily lives. In fact, Art in Igbo land is very spiritual. The gods of the heathen worship, such as "Agwu Isi" and "Ikenga", "Ofo na Ogu" all are priceless works of Art that escaped or survived the European ravaging and attempts at depletion during the scramble for the African continent. The survival of these works of art is largely creditable to the geographic features of the area that constitute Igbo land.

Igbo art is spirit-regarding in that the people use art to tap power from the ancestors and the natural and supernatural forces. There appears to be chances for distortion of proportion in order to achieve the image of the spirits. There is no central authority here, rather an extreme abstraction that conjures an acceptable authority.

The advent of Christianity as well as missionary invasion also threatened the Igbo art, but because of how powerful and deeply rooted in their ancestral beliefs, the Ibos retained control of their destiny. People still wonder how this very rich art remained unknown to Europe and America even till this day. Music, literature, songs are defined in terms of occasion and the appropriateness of purpose.

CHAPTER FOUR

THE NATION STATES

Nigeria is a country in West Africa, and very much considered a gift of the river Niger. It is made up of three major ethnic groups; the Ibo, the Hausa and the Yoruba. Here, an attempt will be made to explain ethnicity or ethnic groups in the context of characteristics, spoken language, customs, and cultures of the different groups of the people, who happen to belong to the same race. A Nigerian can from a distance tell whether the individual he is looking at is an Ibo, Hausa or a Yoruba not necessarily from the clothing attire alone but also the physical attributes, which include height, skin complexion and gait. The individual's name is another red flag to look for if one has difficulty telling whether a Nigerian is from either of the major ethnic groups mentioned. Religion is another factor that helps distinguish between the ethnic groups but the major factor is language.

The Ibos of Eastern Nigeria inhabit an area that stretches from a small enclave west of the River Niger around Asaba to Onitsha, Awka in the north to Nsukka, to Okigwe, and southward to Owerri, to the

Cross River, Bendel and Arochukwu, Afikpo, Ogoja and Abakaliki in the East. Some people may say that the Ibos live in the Southeast part of Nigeria, which will not be completely inaccurate, because the Ibos and the Igbo speaking communities are easily miss-categorized, defined and misidentified. They can be located in the area around the lower River Niger in West Africa.

The Ibo is a large ethnic community and very little is known about how the people came to inhabit their lands. Although fragmented and scattered, they inhabit a recognized geographic area. They share common characteristics and closely related cultural patterns based on similar cults and social institutions. Within these common characteristics the Ibo may be divided into five main cultural groups: a western community, on the west bank of the Niger and around Onitsha; the northern group, around Awka, northward to Nsukka and southward to Okigwe; Owerri and its Environs, the Cross River Ibo, near Bende and Arochukwu; and the Ogoja, who live between Afikpo and Abakaliki.

Some documentation would want us to believe that the Ibos originated in the area about 100 miles north of the current location at the confluence of the Niger and Benue Rivers. History also has it that the first Ibos may have moved onto the Awka-Orlu plateau between four and five thousand years ago, from where this early group expanded and in turn, expanded the Igbo kingdom, before the emergence of sedentary agricultural practices. Our interest is the present location of the Igbo speaking people of Southeastern Nigeria illustrated and highlighted on the map that follow.

Before the establishment of colonial administration in this part of Eastern Nigeria, politics existed in the Igbo land. The largest political unit was the village group. The villages were bound together into clans, all the inhabitants of which descended from a common ancestor. As a result, each cultural group is composed of a hundred clans, which would speak a similar dialect and share certain common customs and traditions. Every Ibo has an immediate, and a more remote allegiance binding him to a wide variety of his fellow. The population of the villages ranged from a minimum of four thousands to a maximum of eight thousands persons, men, women and children. Members of a group share common market-square and meeting place known as the village-square otherwise known as obi. Viewed in some other context, village-square may not appropriately be called "obi" because the word may be specifically assigned to a ruling chief's palace. Well, no chief ever rules any Igbo community. Chieftaincy is a mere title, very respected but has little or no authority. They only have their moments at social events- but are figure heads.

Some villages refer to such open space areas as "mbara" or "obom". Social life in Igbo land is based on the concept of extended family, respect for age, and a real sense of community, primarily organized in the same village settings. There is also a shared deity and ancestoral cults that supports a traditional belief in ancestral descent. Leadership and authority are vested in a council of lineage heads and influential wise and wealthy men. The Ibos are very proud people, respectful of their elders but are not easily intimidated. They believe in social equality but vest no authority on any one individual. It is said that the Ibo does not always acknowledge or pay homage to a ruler or chieftain as central authority. They know that the chief or the ruler exists and has that title but hardly attest to the worth or influence of the authority over their private or individual affairs.

"Igbo ama Eze"

They pledge no allegiance or express high regard to the chief. In other words, Ibos have no centralized chieftaincy, hereditary aristocracy, or kingship customs, as can be found among their neighbors such as Benin, and Yoruba. The daunting responsibility of leadership has traditionally been left to the village councils, which include the heads of lineage, elders, titled men, and women who have established themselves economically within the community. It is possible for an Igbo man, through personal success, to become the nominal head of the council.

IDENTITY

Ibos try to identify themselves by belonging to community groups in the area they reside just as is obtainable in the communities they come from back there in motherland Africa. Such situations have resulted in the formation of numerous organizations here in the United States, and especially in California, where there is Okigwe Family Union of Northern California OFUNC and other ethnic organizations that are non-profit. Sometimes many of the organizations and community groups are dissolved in time to form new ones in effort to resolve the clash of egos or the quest for leadership positions. It is not uncommon for one individual to belong to more than one of these community groups, at least as financially contributing member. Meetings to discuss issues of interest and mandates are held during weekends monthly or as situations may warrant.

CHAPTER FIVE

FARMING

Igbo land is uncommonly rich and fruitful, and produces all sorts of crops and vegetables in abundance. The staple crop is yam, and its harvesting is a time for great celebration. Although other crops such as cassava, cocoa yams, corn and rice are plentiful, almost throughout the year, yam is produced efficiently enough to be exported to neighboring states and outside the country. Pineapples flourish without fertilizer or manure, and grow to the size of the watermelons we find here in the United States of America. Because of plentiful sunshine and adequate rainfall, the pineapples are juicy and sweet. Here one will find the largest variety of spices especially peppers and the world's largest variety of fruits and edible plants. Alligator pepper in particular is a native of the Igbo land and though never used in cooking or spicing food, is almost as important as and eaten with the kola nuts.

The majority of Ibos are farmers. It is no surprise that agriculture is the chief employment of people in Igbo land, and almost everyone until recently. Everyone in the family, including women and children partake in this rudimentary agriculture at different levels and at different times of the year. Ibos delight in cultivating the soil, producing crops and raising livestock and in varying degrees the preparation and marketing of the harvested products. It is said that the "Ibo is habituated to labor from earliest years and everyone contributes the sweat of his brow for the good of all." The benefits of this mode of living cannot be over-estimated. They adopted the saying that idleness is killing and provides a well-equipped workshop for devilish minds. This saying had been elevated to a song in Igbo which implies that working hard will not kill an Ibo man, but idleness does.

> Oru ike a naghi egbu di mkpa, ihe na egbu dimkpa bu e no nkiti, ma o bu noro otu nga were aka abuo fa nyi (fanye) n'ukwu

Early Ibos were yam farmers and oil palm cultivators. With the assistance of migrant labor, they harvested the fruit of the palm tree, which is processed into palm oil, and exported to Europe in fairly large quantities, making it a fairly profitable cash crop. Before venturing into western type jobs and the opportunities education offered, they were also very good artists, sculptors, and had a reputation for being exceptionally enterprising and independent. History by Europeans document that the earliest surviving Igbo art forms were from the 10th century (Igbo Ukwu), and that the fine quality of those copper alloy castings suggest that Igbo society had already achieved a level of technology rivaling contemporary Europeans. Samples of bronze bowls, mortar for grinding and pounding food such as yam and fou-fou and statues are included in this book to illustrate the level of advancement and artistry.

The Ibos are the largest ethnic group of Eastern Nigeria, and primarily inhabit the present Abia, Anambra Imo and the states on their outskirts. Conveniently, the people may be grouped into five cultural divisions: northern (Onitsha), southern (Owerri), western (ika), eastern (Cross River) and northeastern (Abakaliki). Before the British colonized Nigeria the Ibos were not united as a single people but lived in autonomous local communities. The cultural groups have unique ethnic identities that are un-mistakable. Recently, these states in Nigeria have been further divided into smallish several states too numerous to keep count of and incomprehensible to justify, even to the soldiers who did the most recent partitioning of 1998, in the name of state creation. One very distinct example is my home sweet Okigwe which has one of its districts carved into two states, Imo and Abia, respectively. The talk of creating more states continues out of fear on the part of the ruling military personalities that the events leading to the sixties Biafra vs. Nigeria civil war be avoided. The creation of more and more states reduces the chances of one group of people that think alike to belong to same state, by any imagination possible.

The Ibos traditionally farmed for mere subsistence on small pockets of family plots of land. The sale of produce was only necessary when the need for other non-farm products arise. This started during post "trade by barter" period. The main crops sold were cassava, yam, cocoa yam, palm produce (palm oil and palm kernel), corn, maize, tropical fruits and vegetables but the main staples are yam and cassava. There are no fiscal year reports on farm investments. In fact, farmers hardly kept any records of farm earnings and expenditures. Vegetables are cultivated all year round and only the excesses are taken to the open markets and fruit stands to be sold. Such market places are likened to the farmers market found in America. Yams come in about four varieties, but could be more depending on who you ask. Cocoa yam also has four varieties and I have my favorite of the cocoa yams growing up in Okai village in Umuna, Okigwe.

These staple crops thrive on varying soils in different parts of the Igbo land. Around the house and within the courtyards crop rotation is practiced. Organic manure from the dropping of domesticated animals such as goats and other such wastes are used to replenish gardens seasonally that crops and plants continue to do well every year. Rice is cultivated in abundance by very few farmers who do so for commercial purposes. Commercial purposes here means that rice is bagged into large sacs by rice merchants who buy direct from rice farmers, and then sell to rice traders who sell to consumers on retail basis, with differing generally accepted units of measures. The main exports are palm oil and palm kernel. Basically, one can say that the Igbo land flows with rich soil and good weather, but because of high literacy rate many Ibos are civil servants, business entrepreneurs, skilled craftsmen and wage laborers, especially since 1960, when Nigeria gained political independence from Britain.

CHAPTER SIX

IGBO ALPHABETS

The set of letters and characters with which the Igbo language is written are arranged in customary order as the system in English language. This is so because an Ibo man has to be literate to write the Igbo language. In other words, our great grand parents who were not educated had no written Igbo. The absence of written Igbo language made it impossible to have recorded history. What we have is oral history from stories told to our great grand parents who communicated such stories to their children and it continued through the generations until the first generations that were able to put some of the legends on scripted medium. As the English alphabet has twenty-six letters to represent more than forty sounds - from Greek alpha to beta, the Igbo language also has twenty-six letters, but the Igbo letters represent more than one hundred sounds.

Recently, and oddly enough, some Ibos try too hard in their attempts to right the wrongs they now realize were done them by the persons of Europe, by submitting that the people and the language are one and the same. We strongly believe that despite how the name Igbo or Ibo sounds to a foreigner, we know and should be authoritative enough and proud to educate the foreigner that in written language of Central Igbo, Ibo is the people while the language is Igbo. The development that led to writing the Igbo language on paper should be applauded and the Europeans should be given credit for that. A popular Igbo wise saying states that "a child should not bite the finger that feeds him otherwise the consequences will be severe.

" Nwata anaghi ata mkpuru aka na enye ya nri"

Of course the British are not feeding us now for the above adage to apply, but it is as close as it gets when balancing their evils with their good, especially written language capabilities and academics. The evil that the British did was looting on a grand scale, if we must discount their indoctrination and manipulation. If we must agree with those who claim that Ibo derived from amiss-spelling of the word, Igbo and that it was intentional on the part of the European, we must pose the questions as to why we have not changed or determined the right way to spell names of towns such as Awka, Owerri and even Nigeria all these years and nothing is in the works to do so

Ghana for instance was named Gold Coast but at their independence, the country changed its name to Ghana. If Nigeria decided to adopt a name at her independence in 1960, that would have started a movement, at least to question the origin and reasonableness of certain names of towns roads, streets and why individuals still use their baptismal names as their first, and Igbo names as their middle initial. Yea, what is in the name one might ask? Why should Igbo names be designated to middle initials? Why should the baptismal names be sounded higher than our Igbo names? Mbaonu Ojike, Nnamdi Azikiwe, Nwafor Orizu, Chinue Achebe, Chuba Okadigbo, Aguiyi Ironsi, Odumegwu Ojukwu, these are good examples that should have led us to something but eventually there was no proposition to that effect. People like Cyprain Ekwensi never bought it, not K.ingsley Mbadiwe, Michael Okpara, Sam Ikoku,

Francis Akanu Ibiam, Jim Nwobodo and recent proponents of Igbo/ Ibo miss-spelling.

We learned that the name of our country Nigeria was derived from two words Niger area which were combined in describing the location of the land mass on both sides of the River which European explorers, Mongo Park and the Lander brothers found as they made their way into the hinterland of West Africa from the Niger delta, on the Atlantic coast of West Africa. The things our great grand forefathers did not tell us we may question and offer our opinions, as in this situation Igbo vs. Ibo, but then, we must remind ourselves that we are united by a common culture, language, tradition and beliefs, nonetheless.

We accepted Enugu and are yet to question how it should be spelt and what the name implies. One may have a point to believe that ENUGWU should be the correct spelling simply because the heros we worshipped growing up such as Azikiwe or Azukaiwe pronounced or called it Enugwu. It may make an interesting reading to be schooled on what vowel or consonant was left out by design by the European that first wrote Enugu instead of Enugwu or Elu-ugwu, otherwise I am yet to see the relevance, in the argument and controversy over Ibo and Igbo? I was taught that Ibo is the person and Igbo is the language. The same goes for Onitsha. Shouldn't we change it now to ONUSHA or ONUISHA or better yet, ONUCHA because that is how it sounds to us and all the intellectuals of Igbo descent from Azikiwe to Nwafor Orizu, Odumegwu Ojukwu, Cardinal Arinze, Okongwu? We do remember how all those names sound and how the Ibos pronounce them. We may decide to start changing things but should not go it by way of the blame game. Better yet, we may ask what the name means, and if derogatory change it to a more befitting, suitable or appropriate name of an Igbo town.

To really determine what it should be called or be known as may be we have to understand what the word means in Igbo. Okigwe was derived from the topography of the town. The early inhabitants settled in the valley, surrounded by steep hills. When it rained, water washed down the hills alluvium and all that made the valley soil very fertile and rich for farming and cultivation. The area was described as bowl shaped hence oku igwe meaning bowl of the sky.

Umuna, a town in Okigwe derived its name from Mr. Una who was the first man to settle on the southern bank of Imo River about ten miles south of Okigwe main. He had three children, UHI, EZI FOKE AND AKU-NWATA, Together they were called the children of UNA, meaning UMU UNA but written UMUNA. UMU means CHILDREN in Igbo.

Orlu is another interesting name we can quarrel with its spelling. But a good argument could be made by any educated well-meaning Nigerian in regard, if we strongly believe we are being done a disservice. May be one individual is all it takes to start a national debate to change the names of the towns, cities and rivers that were given by colonial Britain because these names make little cultural or national sense to us, before others can jump on the bandwagon to seriously examine the logic and appropriateness for adoption of my submission that Ibo is the people and Igbo is the language, a distinction my teachers impressed on me during my study of the reading and written language during my school days in Igbo land.

Of course, there are other known very pressing issues we should be addressing right about now concerning our fate, but I put that in a deep freezer for my next communication. It is also true that there had been countless Igbo writers and authors, numerous leaders and academicians who could have spoken eloquently on the subject but they did not. Rather, their diction have either been in English language, Literature, other disciplines that might be considered more rewarding, valuable and more enterprising than Igbo language studies. This could be one of the reasons why we do not speak the Igbo language half as frequently even amongst ourselves as other ethnic Nigerians such as the Yoruba person and the Hausa speak their languages.

Ibos embraced the English language better or more than the Yoruba or the Hausa. Some of us, well-meaning Ibos in Europe and the United States of America may some day take our issue on the subject to the literate chieftains back home to examine our claim that we are Igbos not Ibos, and that calling ourselves Ibos or being called Ibos would amount to mixing our identity, name, language just as the colonial intentional misrepresentation had it over the years, before we arrived. The good news is that since none of us would claim to be professor of Igbo language and culture, but are simply providing a service that could fill an all important void. We would humbly stand to be corrected, and open to researched documentation and general acceptance and standard.

The submission here is WE ARE IBOS AND OUR LANGUAGE IS IGBO, so changing and addressing ourselves otherwise may require better equipment, education and qualification. Many of those who read rudimentary Igbo literature books such as Omenuko; Ije Odumodu Jere; Ala Bingo; and Ogbalu - before venturing into various career paths, may now search for those books, and share them with the new generation of Ibo children, so that they can put aside their ipods and play stations game consoles for a family evening together on one of those lazy summer vacations. We desperately need to keep the Igbo language and culture alive, so as to pass them on.

Be it that is made, there are issues that need resolving in or about the Igbo language phonetics, tone-marking, regional varieties as distinguished by features of vocabulary, grammar and pronunciation or sounding the words otherwise known as dialect. Here are some examples:

Some Ibos say "enu" while others say "elu" when we mean "height" or "high" or "up."

Some say "ala" while others say "ani" when we mean "soil" or "land" or down or ground or floor.

Some say "alu emee" while others say "aru emee" when exclaiming that something abominable or worthy of causing disgust, hatred or unpleasant had happened!

The letters "N" and "L" are used in the same manner or means of expression to serve the same purpose depending on the region of the Igbo land we hail from. At the same time it must be stressed here that an Igbo word can not be interpreted to show its meaning until used in a sentence. Just as in English language where one word can be used as a noun or a verb or even as an adjective.

Take for instance: WORK.

I work/she works at the Department of Education (work used as a verb)

She is quite a piece of work (work used as a noun) to say she was not created by god's apprentice.

His work is to assign duties and responsibilities to the incoming freshmen at the State Assembly.

While there could be legitimacy in our choosing to be called African Americans, Black Americans, Afro-Americans or Blacks at any point in our process of finding who we are in America, the Ibo man never lost his identity at any point in our history.

ETHNICITY

Ibos may well be the purest ethnic group of humans that still exist on this planet, in my opinion.

The explorers, the European traders and intruders had limited contacts with the core Ibo communities, because means of travel was by boat through the River Niger delta from the Atlantic Ocean. Even the missionaries who made in –roads beyond the coastal villages primarily were propagating the religious messages they were prevented form spreading in Europe.

Outside influences were limited to education and religion. The teaching of the Igbo language is the most difficult thing to do to non-Igbo speaking people. This is not to say that the teacher would have difficulty delivering the materials but because the learner can not place a distinctive meaning to every word he learns until the word is used in a sentence. There is a central written Igbo language but somehow, dialects do throw in "monkey wrench" from time to time into the spoken word. If one would learn Igbo language from an Ibo man from Orlu, and tries to communicate with a fellow from Owerri, and another individual from Onitsha sits in to offer his interpretation, each will understand what the other is saying but to the non-Igbo, it will appear as if listening to the United Nations. I am quite sure it is equally difficult for the non-son of the soil, meaning an Ibo man born outsider the Igbo land to grasp as we will find out in some of the examples in this book.

CIRCUMCISION

Ibos do not leave their sons intact, that is with the foreskin dangling beyond the eight day after birth. The hood of skin known as foreskin which boys are born with that cover the head of the penis is surgically removed to expose the end of the penis. This is done at the doctor's office or at a licensed midwife's maternity room. Circumcision is painful and for that reason, parents prefer to have it done during the first week when it will heal very quickly. Circumcision is a must in Igbo land and culture. It is a tradition that is always carried out for several reasons. It is believed that a son committed the "original sin" as he passed through the birth canal and must be cleared and cleansed by circumcision. That was the belief unless a son arrived through caesarean.

Circumcised penis is cleaner and easier to clean. In observing a penis with the foreskin intact, urinating goes through a real process by which the foreskin gets filled up first and released from this water balloon type receptacle, from which the urine trickles out. It is never completely emptied because the urine does not have total command of exit. It would constitute real problem for any adult, imagining what would not be completely emptied after a like business.

Daughters were circumcised also till early eighties. The risk of circumcision in sons are never discussed nor is the benefit or the function of the foreskin. The Ibos circumcise their daughter to discourage promiscuity in them. It is called removing the pleasure principle so as to consider child bearing primary essence of the female sex organ. Recently, it is said that daughter be not circumcised. Circumcision may also be based on religious as in cultural beliefs. Opinions are diverse as to whether circumcision has medical benefits, but there is no doubt that cleaning beneath the foreskin would not be as easy as cleaning a circumcised male.

Circumcised females, about ninety-five percent of all Ibo females forty years of age, which would include every Ibo female born before 1970, lose interest in intimate relationships really quickly. To explain this would be too graphic for this family book, but from all indications, very obvious.

The circumcision of the female results in the complete erasure of the only sensitive and responsive pleasure point of the female's sex organ. It is irreversible and for a victim husband, the work of making your wife a woman becomes enormously difficult, and frustrating. The only consolation is child-bearing or if out of pity, your wife pretends to still have something to offer.

This is the reason why most Ibo males function intimately even in their seventies, while the females in their late thirties and early forties complain of being too old, too sleepy, not ready, have a headache, got more important things to do now than to lay around like we just got married. Sometimes their excuses range from her making money; or has a career and that the husband should be happy and be fulfilled for that reason alone; to bad back; my off-days are next tomorrow; and the day after; the kids are not asleep yet; or when I come back from the store.

Circumcision destroys the essence of a woman's femininity that results in a husband's frustration, especially when they are unable to prick the sides of her intent. For the males, circumcision enhances presentation and functionality among other benefits, while the uncircumcised may likely feel inferior or inadequate, and a turn-off for the prospective partner due to personal hygiene, or even on religious grounds

CHAPTER SEVEN

EDUCATION

Education in Igbo land is a process of developing mentally in acquiring knowledge, which involves teaching and learning. The West on the other hand, defines education as the knowledge and development that result from educational process. A person's manners and up-bring may or may not have much to do with formal education. If one is well educated, he or she is respected and expected to be intelligent and knowledgeable. He is also expected to make a living and live above means.

"Onye oke akwukwo" or onye gutara akwukwo or "Onye guru akwukwo"

"Bukuru man" in pigin English

"Akwukwo" when used in Igbo sentence can mean a host of things depending on the language structure and usage, but mainly connote knowledge and learning in terms of education, but specifically mean book. Education may also mean "oke mmuta"

ENGLISH	IGBO
Book	Akwukwo
Intelligence	Ogugu isi / amam ihe
Knowledge	Mmuta
School	Ulo akwukwo
School	Ulo mmuta

The educational system in Igbo land was patterned after the British, with classroom activities structured in a way that the teacher does the teaching and all the talking, while the students or pupils listen attentively and learn. Students' participation in class is through question and answer method. By rule, the student raises up his hand over his head when he wants to ask a question, and stands up to speak if allowed to do so by the teacher. If the teacher notices that a student is not attentive in class, he would call on the student to pay attention but if the student is caught a second time goofing off, the teacher may ask the student to come to the front of the class and share his knowledge of the topic discussed. Classes are taught in English language starting from the elementary grades.

Only in the pre-school and kindergarten grades are pupils taught in the vernacular, which is Igbo language. The school system emphasizes academic courses throughout the elementary and primary grades, with a little bit of arts and crafts and physical education.

Subjects that are taught in elementary and primary grades include:

English language
Geography
Mathematics
History
Sciences
Bible knowledge

While at school, students go outside to play and partake in Physical Exercises and Handiwork Craft practices for an hour each weekday respectively, but these are not taught as subjects on which to earn grades for graduation. During (P.E) students engage in activities such as playing soccer, tennis, basketball and volley ball. Handiwork periods engage students in activities such as basket making, carving, and broom making. These crafts and handiwork products of students are examined, judged and graded each month by the respective classroom teachers, sold or auctionedand the proceeds used for end of year parties or put in general funds. The major difference between United States educational system and what a foreigner will see in Igbo land is that students who fail to make the grades are retained in such grades until they earn the passinggrades. A student can be asked to repeat a class for as long as it takes the student to pass the class.

I can still remember a student who repeated the eighth grade for four years before he was promoted to the ninth grade. In fact, the situation was not unique, and there are no interventions or litigation resulting from students being retained in their previous classes when their age groups have moved on. On completion of primary school education, each student receives the First School Leaving Certificate.

SECONDARY (HIGH) SCHOOL

The Secondary school grade levels are the grade when many schools are co-educational, and have uniforms for different school activities and functions – uniforms for classroom lectures, separate uniforms for church services, after school dormitory wear and different one for physical exercises. Final year students also are issued with school blazers to differentiate them from under class and junior students. Secondary school education usually lasts for five years, and studentchoose eight subjects to offer in the West African Examination Council final. This is a comprehensive exit examination that determines your distinction or the lack there of, irrespective of how well the student may have perceived his performance in high school. This final examination could propel a student to the best university in Nigeria or may disappoint to a point of dashing a young man's hopes and dreams of academic pursuit. Secondary school in Nigeria and especially in Igbo land is the equivalent of the high school system that operates in the United States of America, which starts form the ninth grade to twelfth grade.

Recently in California USA parents and lawmakers were debating whether or not "Exit Examinations" are fair to "minority" students in neighborhood schools. This is ridiculous because Exit examinations ought he grounds for graduation from high school. It should not be politicized so students could look forward to it and graduate if they pass the examination. Arguing otherwise would strengthen the misconception that some people are inferior to others right from birth.

In Nigeria, when I was in secondary school, exit examination was mandatory. The examination was conducted and administered by a separate body from school districts and even the country. This was called W.A.E.C which is short for West African Examination Council, head-quartered in Accra Ghana. A second exit examination was called G.C.E, otherwise known as General Certificate of Education, head quartered in London England. During those days, if a high school student fails to earn a pass in English language and Mathematics, he or she is referred to retake the examination and will not be awarded High School Diploma. It is silly, in my opinion to believe that the introduction of exit examinations for graduating classes will remedy the academic problems in our K to 12 grade school system. Forty years later, California is embracing Exit Exam, just to show what type of emphasis the system placed on education and learning in Nigeria

We promote students from class to class till they reach the 12th grade and all of a sudden, we impose the almighty Exit Examination. What do we expect when we believe in age-appropriateness as criterion for sitting a warm body in a class-room. If a pupil is unable to learn the alphabets A, B, to Z, and numerals 1, 2, 3, to 10 or unable to master the course load in the curriculum approved for kindergarten, does it matter if the child is 5, 6 or 7 years old, and has not performed fairly, he or she has to remain in kindergarten until he or she is capable of learning anything beyond that to be considered for promotion to first grade.

Children miss out if promoted to a new class each year irrespective of how ill – prepared they are for new learning if the only consideration for promotion is age, political correctness not withstanding. Also drawing from experience while growing up in Nigeria, if the educational system continues to dump all students in new classes each year, on the basis of age appropriate clause, then these students may not be told that the rule of the high school game has changed now that they are about to make their exit from secondary school.

Exit Examination politics will in the future damage the education system as Affirmative Action politics destroyed opportunities for the genuinely deserving minority candidates. The privileged in the American system unfairly, or should I say, by insidious means use the Affirmative Action clause to their advantage. Even those in favor of Affirmative action never did their research well to be capable of knowing whom affirmative action favored, in my honest opinion. Women became the only minority that fulfilled the federal clause in regard but when one case of admission to law school crops up, the issue becomes that of black and white student applicants.

The active effort to improve the employment or educational opportunities of minority groups and women turned out to be another effort for the privileged to justify putting their relatives in thefeminine kind in employment positions that called for minority groups and women. Educational opportunities also went that way and fewer and fewer minorities were helped by affirmative action, in my opinion, except in token situations. The system redefined the affirmative actiondefinition. Affirmative action ultimately turned out to be an active effort to improve the employment or educational opportunities of member of white female groups and a few token minority women. This is my opinion because any organization where a minority is needed to reflect somehow the chemistry or representative nature of the structure of that entity, a white woman is brought in to fulfill that federal requirement. In turn, their well-placed husbands argue that blacks have benefited from Affirmative action, or that Affirmative action is unfair to whites.

Need we discuss Small business loan, Minority business loans and how or who qualifies for them? I guess not. It is wrong for the decision to graduate from high school to come down from a judges, otherwise the United States will continue to look overseas for their engineers, scientists, doctors, researchers, teachers, programmers and authors. The rationale for this brief comment is justifiable, since Ibos live in this society, and our children have no other country than this United States of America, no matter how we kid ourselves about going back to Nigeria to live or retire.

CHAPTER EIGHT

CONSONANTS AND VOWELS IN IGBO ALPHABETS

A E I O U

These are vowels as we know them, and barely change in written Igbo language.

CONSONANTS

B, D, F, G, H, J, K, L, M, N, NY, P, R, S, T, U, V, W, Y, Z

The "NY" consonant has two distinctive pronunciations and uses in spoken Igbo language.

ENGLISH
A B C D E F G H I J K L M N O P Q R S T U V W X Y Z

IGBO
A B GB CH D E F GW GH I J KW L M N NY O KP Q R
SH T U V W Y Z

IGBO CONSONANTS
B, D, F, G, H, J, K, L, M, N, NG, NY, P, R, S, T, U, V, W, Y,
Z.

AUXILIARY CONSONANTS
GB, KP, SH, CH, GW, GH, KW, NW, NY.

Deceptively, these alphabets look alike but they are sounded very differently, some are tone-marked, some should have lines above them for differentiation, while others are written with characters foreign to western type-writers or computer key boards.

Example: E ga a nu mmiri?

Would you like to drink water?

A polite question asking if one would like to drink water, the 'N' in 'nu' is written with a hyphen above it. 'Nuo' is written with a hyphen above the N, (and a period or dot below the o) to convey meaning.

Tone-marking is used in written Igbo language because a word may mean or imply several meanings. The same can be said of the English language too.

In English language, 'hawk' can be a noun for any of the various birds of prey known to have strong hooked beaks, powerful feet with long claws, or as a transitive verb to describe carrying goods around and offering them for sale at public unregulated places, and also as an intransitive verb to describe an old lady clearing her throat noisily. There is no differentiation in the manner hawk is written in English.

The orthographic system of Igbo language is difficult. For this reason, a person foreign to Igbo land may think that the language is hard to learn. Far from that, any foreign language is difficult to learn, unless one approaches it at very early age. Knowledge of the Igbo language is important but not a requirement for understanding the people, their culture and their unique heritage.

English language is spoken or understood by all Ibos, at all corners of the land, though at different levels of diction and that makes translation easy and fun. Interest in the language is of preponderant importance. In written Igbo language, for example 'akwa' is tone-marked to show differences in meaning.

akwa means bed	(something on which one sleeps or rests)
"akwa" means cry	(weep or shed tears)
akwa means egg	(laid by the female of a bird)
akwa means cloth	(material made by weaving of cotton, wool, silk, linen)

Another example where tone-marking makes the difference is 'EZE'

EZE means Teeth	(of tooth)
EZE means 'King	(Queen/chief (ruler of a town)
EZE' means Avoidance	(keep away from; caution)

Some words are not usually tone-marked and as such have different meanings depending on usage.

Example: 'Guo' can mean read or count.
Guo umuaka ole soro nne ha bia nzuko taa.
(Count the number of children that accompanied their
    mothers to today's gathering)
Guo akwukwo gi gusia ya ike (read your book/study hard)

However, 'Guo' is written with a dot or an underscore for 'u' and 'o' to emphasize the 'or' sound.

During the 1980s while studying and pursuing undergraduate degree at Southern University, Baton Rouge, Louisiana, I sat near a few Iranian schoolmates in the school library. I noticed for the first time that these students were writing some form of messages to their folks in the Middle East in a language that did not require alphabets. I was amazed as these students were writing from right to the left of the sheet of their writing pad. They used only signs and I later was told it was Arabic form of communication. Since then I have been thinking to myself, what if I write my parents in Igbo language? What would be their reaction if they opened the letter and I am asking them to send my remittance, but this time they discover that I wrote them completely in Igbo language? I bet they would not be proud that they are paying so much money for me to study in America, only to have me go there to perfect my native language. What they would have loved to receive a letter from a son in whom they are investing their hard currency in foreign exchange to come down with such jaw-breaking words that would send chills down their spines. That is how bad the British indoctrination is on the Ibo man and his language.

Foreigners who visit Nigeria and want to enter into business with the Ibos have enormous advantage because they would not encounter any language problems since almost everyone speaks and communicates in English, and all contracts are scribbled in English language too. Shops and supermarket shelves are stocked with food items labeled in English. So what is the main reason foreigners and especially African Americans do not want to discover Igbo land. With the end of apartheid in southern Africa, and globalization, Southeastern Nigeria should not be isolated. If they ask the right questions and want someone they can trust I am sure they will find many Ibos waiting with open arms. What is good for India and all those tiny villages in Napal, Bangladesh, Singapore, and recently Eastern Europe could help lift Umuna Okigwe, Mbaise, Oguta, Nekede, Uturu, Agwu, or even Umudike Okwe in Onuimo LGA. In Onuimo LGA of Imo State, Okai village in particular holds the most potential in all of Okigwe because of large endowment of undisturbed land, water and ample supply of human resource. Crude oil drilling should not be the only preoccupation of the West.

CHAPTER NINE

IBOS WHO ARE PUBLISHED WRITERS

Igbo writers delight in publishing in English language. Authors such as Chinue Achebe, Cyprain Ekwensi, all have written in English language but never in Igbo. This makes economic sense, but one can always bet that these great writers, most possibly have spoken more words in Igbo, more eloquently, than in English language. Undoubtedly, English language has helped them pen their way to the pinnacle of their professions, hence their rationale for neglecting their birthright.

Another reason why Igbo writers favor doing so in English is because anyone who can read Igbo literature can read English as well. It is also easier to write in English language than to contemplate doing so in Igbo language. Although English alphabets do not so much differ from the Igbo, they are much faster to write. Then again, most Ibos measure education by how eloquently one expresses himself in English language. If an educated Ibo man chooses to discuss any topic of interest in Igbo, the locals interpret it to mean that the speaker is probably more comfortable in the local language than in the English.

Dr. Nnamdi Azikiwe, in 1957, speaking on the contributions of Church Missionary Society, Bishop Crowder and the translation of the bible into Igbo language, had this to say about our language: "Igbo language is as grammatical as any written language; It has etymology, orthography, prosody and syntax." This I very much agree with, totally, that is why attempts are made here to translate some sentences in both languages so that the reader will not search too hard to understand what is being said as he reads along.

BODY PARTS

IGBO	ENGLISH
Aka	Hand
Anya	Eyes
Afo	Stomach/belly
Azu	Back
Eze	Teeth
Ekwu	Neck
Olu	Neck
Mbo	Nail
Isi	Head
Ihu	Face
Ire	Tongue
Imi	Nose
Otele	Hip
Okpukpo	Bone
Onu	Mouth
Opkoro-Ukwu	Leg
Mkpuru-ukwu	Toes
Ntutu	Hair
Ukwu	Waist
Otu nzo ukwu	one stride

Ikpere (eekpere)	knee
Onu-mmiri	Saliva
Asu	spit
Anya-mmiri	tears

Igbo people value education very highly and children are taught about the parts of the body in English language as they start school. The first person a preschooler learns is the headmaster. It is only when a child leaves primary school that he learns that headmaster is the same title as principal of a school. Nothing puts an Ibo man to shame than to be told that he was unable to put his child through school. Parents of educated children feel mighty proud especially when their children speak English language in public very well. It is like seeing your child hit home run at a little league baseball game. The story spreads like a wild fire in the community.

CHAPTER TEN

BASIC MANNERS

Igbo customs have acceptable social conduct or rules of conduct that ought to prevail for one to be considered conforming to the mode of acting. This customary mode of adherence or peculiarity is characterized often by unconscious mode of action bearing treatment. Table manners may be the most written because foreigners may want not to offend or disgust prospective business partners. Also because manners dictate social conduct and behavior, a foreigner can readily get a crash-course in manners of a people at dinner tables.

AT TABLE DURING MEALS

Hands are thoroughly washed before and after each meal regardless of whether or not you are using your fingers, knife, fork or spoon. You must wash both hands, because customarily the Ibos do not believe in the "glass being half full and/or half empty" sentiment or wise talk. In fact there is an adage in Igbo language which says that one hand by it's self is never washed clean. That the right hand must wash the left as the left washes the right in order for both hands to be clean.

Aka nri kwuo aka ekpe, aka ekpe kwuo aka nri

There are not too many ceremonies before meals. A elderly person or any one he appoints says grace, and diner is served. In middle class families, when meals are presented, spoons, forks and knives are placed utensil end on the plate, handle end on the table. When you have finished eating, you indicate by placing the silverware across the middle of the plate. If a sizable quantity of the food is not eaten, then it is polite to place the utensil end on the plate and the handle end on the table, just as when you commenced eating. Silverware is used for many food items and dishes, with the fork in the left hand, to jab at slices of fried ripe plantains, fish or meat. The prongs or tines of the fork are used to jab and bring the piece of food to the mouth in such way that the food does not fall off before reaching the intended destination. This is quite an art that has been perfected over generations that bibs and aprons are never used at meals, necessarily.

During meals, the most useful utensils are the fork and spoon. Knives are there just to show that you have all that is required to set up a table, and occasionally when big chunks of meat are to be sliced. When you finish eating, you place your fork and spoon with tines resting on the plate. If your plate is completely empty, then you can place your silverware in the middle of the plate.

If you dine as a guest in someone's home, you may leave a small quantity of food when you have finished eating, otherwise you will be served some more food. But if you know that you are not going to finish a plate of food served you, be sure to eat from one corner of the plate. You must not jump around the plate, but if you do, the food will be thrown away. Children from neighboring houses may be offered your left-over, if the food is still presentable, but if you were all over the food even a starving child will not eat it, and food will be thrown away or offered to the dogs.

At a social gathering such as ceremony or festive event, a table is set up with a variety of foods. You will be expected to pick up a plate, proceed to the table and serve yourself. Drinks will also be in plain view so that you will choose the type of food you would prefer. Traditionally females consume soft non-alcoholic drinks in the public such as juices, soda and water. Men have little restriction except when their wives are around and impose of some restrictions, but such is done as whisper in their husbands' ears and politely too.

When at table for tea and breakfast, serving dishes, cups and condiments are not passed around very much. People reach for what is closest to them otherwise you are considered rude and ill-mannered. You also run the risk of brushing the sleeves of your shirt against a teacup you may not use, or a slice of bread you expect someone else to eat. Sometimes a family eats directly from one large tray of food or plate, depending on how close, and the type of food. You do not place your elbows on the table during meals or when any one is eating at the table.

DESSERTS

Desserts consist mainly of fruits, freshly picked from the farm or gardens around the house and washed thoroughly in cold water. Ibos are never in a hurry when eating, and most conversations take place as people relax and enjoy desserts after meals. Ibos do not mix fruits with drinks because it is said that both have different taste buds to satisfy.

"akpiri utara abughi akpiri ji"

When desserts are served, people have enough of it and would love to save drinks for another time otherwise it would amount to wasting food. Ripe juicy pineapples, oranges, guava, cashew fruits, paw-paw, coconuts, mango are the delight of this tropical Igbo land. Pears and mangoes are seasonal fruits and are also enjoyed as desserts. It is difficult to do justice to their description on paper. You have to taste a good really ripened pear when roasted on warm fire-sprinkled ashes, or soaked on slightly look-warm water, to have been there and back. Fruits ripen on trees in the glow of bright sunshine. Trees grow on natural soil and their fruits are not transported long distances to reach final consumers, or sprayed with chemical preservatives, or spiked with artificial colors before they arrive at our dinner tables. Your mouth tells you how delicious nature intends fruits to be if you taste some in the Igbo land.

EATING OUT - HOTELS AND RESTAURANTS

Ibos like to cook their own food unless when they are out on trips and very far away from home. The habit of eating out was ridiculed until recent years. For non-overnight trips a man is expected to go home and eat what his wife had prepared for him. The wife always fixes large meals as she awaits the husband's return. Well, that is the way it is in Igbo land today that was the way it was and had been, but the way it is as a wife flies west of the Atlantic Ocean to the United States could be as different as daylight and darkness. During the course of the meal, the husband updates the wife on how his day had been. It will be deemed disrespectful of the wife in Igbo land if a man comes home and on being presented his dinner, tells his wife that he is already full, or not hungry. You just do not say it or even think about it.

In Igbo land it was a taboo to find a young lady near a restaurant, hotel or a motel, so if spotted, the young lady is considered wayward, irresponsible or belonging to the oldest profession. If a young man is seen eating in a restaurant within twenty mile radius from his home, he is considered as having problem in his house or mapping out a dirty secret from the family. He is called sensuous. Ibos go home to eat dinner, and do not stop for a bite for any reason.

> nwoke ori ofe oma or nwoke onu uto – someone who likes to eat in hotels.

Such a man, it is believed, thinks that his wife's cooking is not tasty enough to satisfy him. If such is the case, the man is to be blamed because he is charged with the responsibility of providing for the family and making sure his provision is adequate for his family.

> "Good soup na money mekam"

If a woman's soup is delicious, it is evidence that the husband provided plenty of money for the wife to have purchased enough ingredients.

Food is freshly prepared daily in local utensils such as pots, mortar, baskets, trays and eaten with spoons, paddle and finger tips. Below is an example of a kitchen tool for preparing pounded yam, and fou-fuo which is the main dinner dish of a typical Ibo family on each given night. Pots could be made out of clay or steel or aluminum.

MORTAR AND PESTLE (OKIRI OR IKWE AND AKA IKWE)

WOODEN MORTAR FOR GRINDING

Condiments such as pepper, pumpkin, melon, achi, ukpo, uzuzara, ayoro, utazi are ground in wooden mortar as the one above. These are ingredients for soup preparation. The Igbo soup is unlike the soup the western world is familiar with. Soup is never canned. It is prepared from scratch with fish, meat, fresh vegetables and thickenings the thought of it here makes me hungry.

The most popular (ODO) Grinder in Igbo land

Wooden mortar carved out of (osisi orji) iroko tree. Iroko tree should not be mistaken for cotton tree (osisi apu) both grow into huge trees but the stronger tree is the former. Wooden mortar of the type immediately above may also be carved out of oil bean tree, the hardest of them all.

CHAPTER ELEVEN

MUSICAL INSRUMENTS

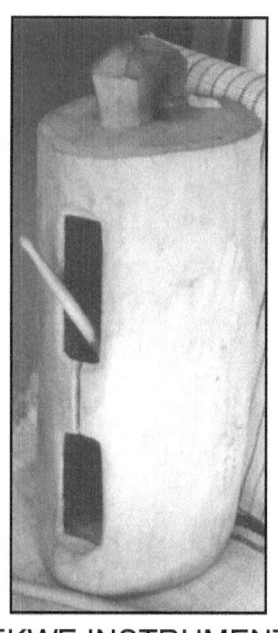

EKWE INSTRUMENT

Ekwe has no English translation. It is not a drum, but more or less a wooden bell. It features greatly as an alarm system, in summoning the village and town to very important occasions, to Church service, and even to announce the death of a Christian Church member. It is also a major equipment for the masquerade culture. When it sounds, it can be heard across towns, miles away.

UDU – IGBO PERCUSSION POT

Udu is a vessel drum that originated form the Igbo people of Nigeria. It is a percussion pot which traditionally was a water jug with another holein the side. It features prominently at ceremonial music, played by women

The makers through the years have discovered how to get better sounds from the Udu, by use of different types and texture of clay soil. Today, Udu is used and heard all over Nigeria and in the western world.

GOURD RATTLE (OYO)

Gourds have been used as storage containers for food, water, palm wine and as musical instruments. They are also made into beautiful decorative works of art. It is also called calabash – a dried one surrounded by seeds to make percussion instrument rattle, hence called gourd rattle.

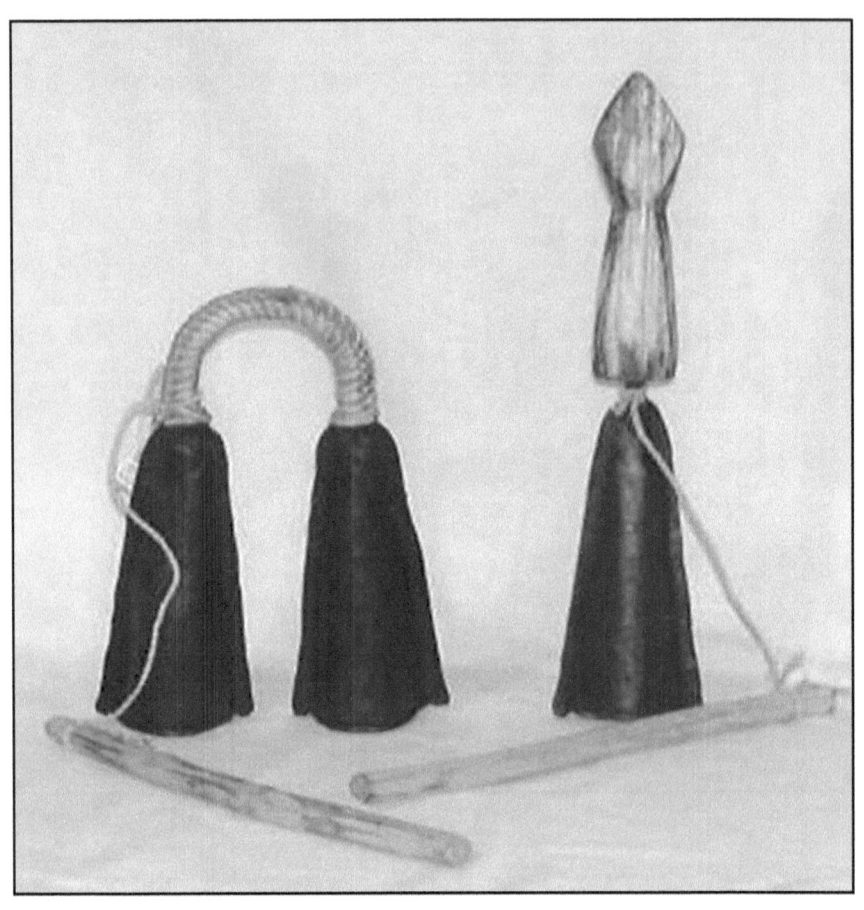

OGENE MKPI N'ABU – TWIN GONGS

CHAPTER TWELVE

ART AND FESTIVITIES

Igbo art can be described as reflecting a world view that is active and energetic, forceful and constantly in motion, and even aggressive. While the English defines art as the conscious use of skills and creative imagination especially in the production of beautiful objects. In Igbo language, art is more appropriately described as the creative power, ingenuity and expertness in workmanship. Igbo art includes activities carried out by both men and women. Pottery, metalworking, carving, decorating, drawing, basket making crafts, dancing and masquerade are forms of art in Igbo land. Igbo art not only interprets human experience, it has been a product of an age of faith, with the gifted artist primarily concerning himself with the spiritual content of his product. An Ibo man grows up learning every aspect of the Igbo art and culture. For generations, woodcarvers have made statues and masks for use in ceremonies, home decorations and shrines.

While woodcarving is still done today in Igbo land, very little of it possess the power of earlier carvings. The trade is no longer passed down the generations as before and the young generations though may cherish these wood carvings, they would rather purchase them than sit down to exhibit the dedication and patience that is required to learn and master the art. Art carving if still done but few of the products possess the power of earlier carvings.

Masquerade procession during festival - Orlu Imo State
(Ekpe festival as portrayed in an article by
Prof. Ivor Miller- DePaul Univ.)

IGBO FESTIVAL
(Picture supplied by Kingsley Ezenekwe - bbc media/images)

An Ibo dancer at a celebration of New Yam Festival in Abia State-Nigeria

ART COLLECTIONS

There are no private art collections among Ibos but there are personal art objects, the likes of which you cannot find in New York or London.

IGBO UKWU CULTURE BRONZE BOWL - 9TH/10TH CENTURY A.D.

IKENGA STATUE - KEPT IN SACRED AREA

KENGA; OPARA OGU; DURU-UHI; OFO; AMADI-OHA OTA-NKWU; ALA-UKWU; OGWUGWU
Picture by: Obu Udeozo (Feb. 14, 2002) Jos, Nigeria

The Ikenga Statue is found and kept in sacred shrines of the Igbo speaking people of Southeastern Nigeria. Ikenga is believed to possess a protective spirit and to provide success, achievement and accomplishment. The word "ikenga" translates to place of strength.

These are a few rare art objects that are still symbolic adaptations of several Igbo heathen gods.

In Amadi's (1973) play, Isiburu, the actor performs such rituals to solicit the guidance and protection of the gods of the land. Such rituals are performed at different occasions and places, most of the time in the shrines of the gods which house their carved images.

Visitors to Igbo land are often in shock to see pieces of art marvels and artifacts that are not accorded any particular value on account of age alone. Interestingly enough one powerful reason given for non-preservation of these rare art products is not to compromise the impulse to repeat the process. In the words of a famous Ibo author Chinue Achebe,"the Igbo choose to eliminate the art product and retain the process so that every generation receives its own impulse and kinesis of creation"

WATER SPIRIT MASK – IGBO ART

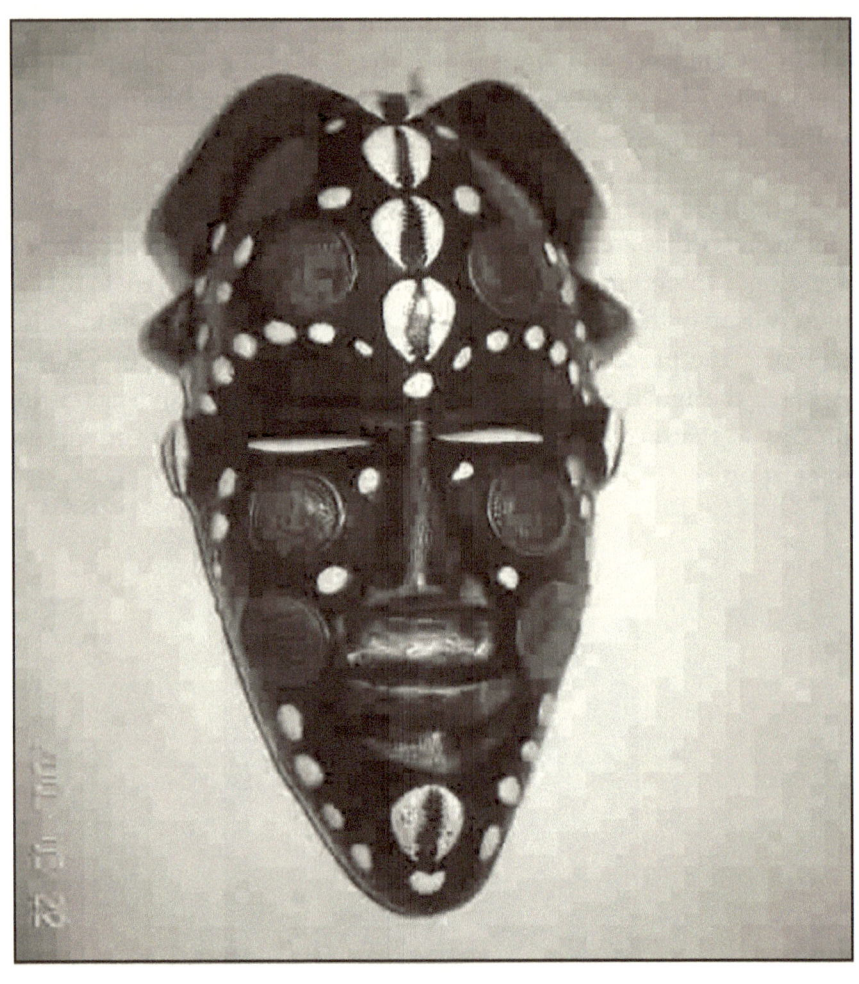

IGBO MASK DECORATED WITH COWRIES
(Photo:

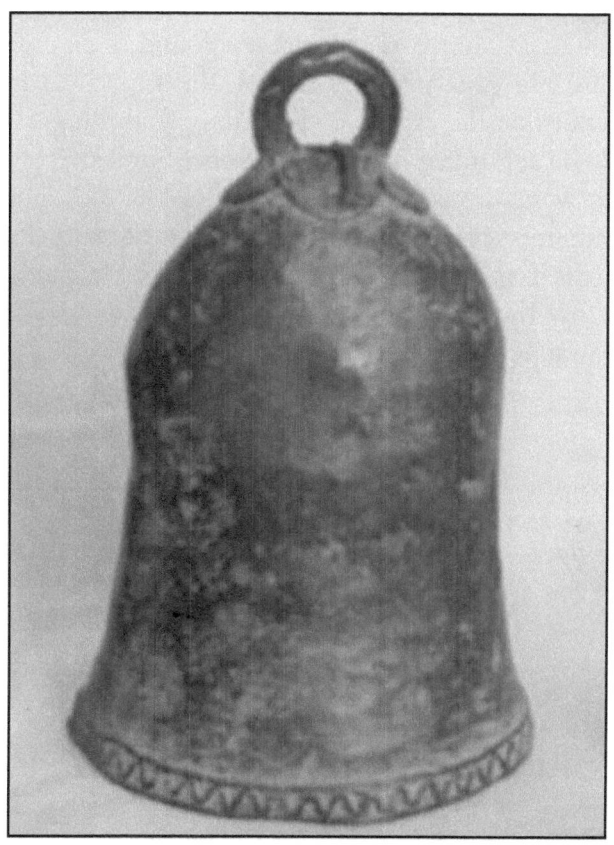

Earliest corpus of Nigerian Bronzes unearthed in the Igbo interior Igbo-Ukwu- a northern Igbo country-side in Southern eastern Nigeria hoop and thin cast vessels, small bronze bells provided with clapper.

Photo: africart.yourbusinesstips.com

Igbo-Ukwu features prominently in this chapter because, as mentioned earlier, Igbo history is mainly oral history so any documentation of Igbo Art will make interesting authoritative reading. An article captioned "Nigerian Bronze Bells" – Sunday March 19, 2006 by John Fagalde, reads in part: "Southwestern Nigeria is the home of the Yoruba and Bini traditions and was originally thought to be the sole source of the wealth of bronze castings, and so it was with great interest that a new source of material was found in an archaeological sight beyond the eastern shores of the Niger." "It is here in the IGBO interior that the earliest corpus of Nigerian Bronzes have been unearthed", he continued. In the course of controlled excavation over 100 bronzes were brought to light at IGBO-UKWU, among which were large numbers of vessels and other artifacts bronze bells decorated with tiny coiled spirals, miniature human heads, leopards, serpents, floral patterns. The bells were said to typify small and some elaborate designs of Southern Nigerian Collections.

NEW YAM FESTIVAL IN IGBO LAND
IGBO ART "Christian grave with anger" - World history sources

A VILLAGE WOMAN WEAVING BASKET –
AN IMPORTANT IGBO CRAFT

Baskets are made from mid-ribs of mature palm fronds. It is a craft that is passed on from generation to generation. Baskets serve immense purposes even in today's Igbo society, for siffing fermented cassava, processing tapioca, for starch, for picking garden fruits and vegetables, for transporting farm produce to long distances, for holding food and flowers.

"Igbo music serves as spiritual communication, storytelling, calling to prayer, for ceremonial gatherings and healing, and to induce trance states or to dispel negative attitudes or psychological trauma. Igbo music accompany dancing or highlight such festive occasions as rites of passage, harvest and other social events." - Onye Onyemaechi – (1999)

MASQUERADES & THE MEN DIRECTLY INVOLVED DURING NEW YAM FESTIVAL

MASQUERADES

Masquerade (Mmanwu or Igbada Mmuo) is a thing of beauty, the dance, the music, the atmosphere surrounding the appearance at any occasion, all epitomize the richness of the Igbo culture artistically. It represents the Igbo art in it's entirety, judging from the sculptor on the head of the masquerade, the music that combines rhythm, jazz, and blues in it's originality, the painting, the costume, the drama and the gaiety in the magnificent performance of the masquerades. The different instruments and devices the Ibo uses to produce music (drums, gongs, bells, flutes, etc.) all communicate to the masquerade, the spectators, the spirits, and the ancestors. When the masquerade moves, it dances, and every of its' artistic display radiates energy that is instantly transmitted to the spectators. Masquerades exhibit elaborate dance routines which are constantly in motion and to enjoy the spectacle, one has to be spiritually into it, and following the ever evolving process. A popular Igbo adage describes this inherent appreciation of the masquerade this way:

"Anaghi a no otu nga elekiri mma-nwu"

"Anaghi a no otu ebe ekiri mmanwu"

Anaghi a no ofu ebe ekiri mmanwu

The above three Igbo sentences are the same and convey the same meaning, basically saying it in three different dialects that one can not fully enjoy the masquerade from a single vantage point.

Masquerades do not just dance, they choreograph, gesture, communicate with the drums and flutes, relate direct, admonish the instrumentalists and acknowledge spectators as they perform routines and dances. This is the reason the Ibos strongly believe in the above proverb that one does not stand in one place to watch and enjoy a masquerade. Masquerading is the art of giving life to a mask. One visitor to the Igbo event described in his book that "Masquerade is the representative form of African indigenous theater." In the words of Chinue Achebe, "the dance of the Masquerade is an artistic deployment of motion." and that "the dance and the masquerade appear to have satisfied the Igbo artistic appetite most completely." Masquerade is said to represent reincarnated spirits of the ancestors.

CHAPTER THIRTEEN

ATTRACTING ATTENTION

Hey!, Hei!, which could be another way of saying "hello you" or "hi there" can be used to call on someone or to attract attention. In an effort to appear more polite, one can say "excuse me" as some Igbo dialects are spoken with a mixture of "broken English" type speak.

Di anyi ! (sounded De), meaning "my man" or "our man"

Di anyi ! is also an abbreviated form of "nwoke di anyi" also a manner of addressing a man, if you want to talk to him or have something to say to him. – a way of attracting attention.

When people are sitting around and you want to ask a question and you are not familiar or not quite sure of the person's name, you could use one of the following words:

Hello, hey, Mr., nne, di-anyi , nna etc.

These are used if the individual is some distance away from you. Sometimes "hey" is hardly differentiable as English or Igbo word. This is like I said above, some Igbo language words are mixed up with what is known as Pigin English or broken English. Broken or pigin English is socalled because in their use, sentences hardly obey the rules of grammar, such as tenses. This mixture affords a blurred line between English and Igbo language that we characterize it as Engl-I gbo. (a combination of Igbo and English – in casual acquaintances). This is to say that Ibos use a combination of Igbo and English to communicate theirs, regardless of their educational levels.

To attract the attention of a friend or family member of the same age group, the Ibo man or woman accomplishes that by calling out their names. As a general unwritten rule, you must use soft or polite tone otherwise annoyance could be easily detected in your tone of voice, and could be interpreted as a command, unless you are commanding the individual. Commanding or harsh tone of voice could only be used for that purpose on a junior person, or an unfriendly person who fails to accord you the respect you have earned or deserve. Example:

English	Igbo
What are you doing?	Gini ka i na eme
What is wrong with you?	O bu gini na eme gi
Are you drunk?	I nuru gbaa n'imi
Are you tipsy/ intoxicated?	Mmanyi o na egbu gi
Are you crazy?	O bu isi mmebi ka i na aria

Polite manner of asking for favor:

Please flag down a taxi for me	Biko, kpora m taxi
Could you fetch me a bottle of water?	I nwere ike kutara
m mmiri	
Stop what you are doing!	Kwusi ihe i na eme

Mr. or Nnaa for men and Miss/Madam or Nne for women, may be used to attract attention of someone either close or far away from you, in a friendly manner. When asking for a favor or you need information, your request must be politely constructed and presented. If one's intention is to ask for information or assistance from a person one knows, one must address the person as Mr. or Miss, followed by the last name (surname) The Ibo man likes to be addressed as "honorable" if he has held an elective office for a day, be it at the local council level. If an Ibo man earns an engineering degree, even if it is an Associate degree from a two-year post secondary school institution, he wants to be addressed as "Engineer" and from my experience nothing else will do.

Big ego, and lawyers, barrister even though all they do for three years is study cases and come out to parade themselves as lawyers. I am not mad at them but in my opinion, it is ridiculous for someone to spend three or four years in college and come out to call himself a lawyer, and barrister, even before passing the bar examination, but you must give them that.

A titled person has to be addressed accordingly and elected officials too otherwise your stance may be considered aggressive and confrontational, and may irritate the impatient ego.

If you meet someone informally, such as in the streets or at public places, there is no culturally definitive way of attracting the person's attention.

A street vendor may be addressed by his wares, such as fruit vendor, so is bus driver, taxi driver, cyclist, biscuits seller and so forth.

Hey! mango seller	Onye mango;
Palm oil seller	Onye mmanu ;
Bread seller	Onye bread;
Orange seller	Onye oroma or oloma

Sometimes hissing sound like "pssss" is enough to make a street hawker or vendor to turn your direction because it is a hustling world out there, in the streets of the big cities. Turn over of their wares is very important to them and as a result, more than one seller might. run to you and try to persuade you to purchase from them. They do not mean any harm, and you should not feel threatened or turned off. They are only trying to make a sale.

CHAPTER FOURTEEN

DAYS

Day	Ubochi
Today	Taa
Yesterday	Unyaahu
Tomorrow	Echi
Week	Izu
Month	Onwa
Year	Afo

There is a difference between Izu ukwu and Izu uka

Izu ukwu represents an 8 day week

Izu uka represents a 7 day week

Izu nta connotes a 4 day week.

In Igbo culture, there are four market days in a week.

NKWO
EKE
ORIE
AFO (AFOR)

There are three types of weekdays in Igboland. The four day week is called "Izu nta which means small week The eight day week is called "izu ukwu" which means big week The seven day week is called "izu Uka" which is the calendar weekIzu nta is specifically used to track the market days. In an eight days week, some of the market days come more than once and it is never a mistake.

BAD LUCK DAY

Afo means market day Nkwo means the day after Afo market Orie means a day to prepare and select the farm produce to sell at Afo market. Eke day is considered in some parts of the Igbo land as a "bad luck" day.

It is the least favored day for an Ibo man to undertake a venture such as initiating a marriage proposal. Religion has somehow changed some of the myth but one is considered gambling with fate if such misconception is not heeded. Quite a few bad omens are believed to happen to people on "Eke" days even to the most deeply religious people.

Just as Americans attribute Friday the 13th as bad luck day, or the day one has to be extra careful, the Ibos blame most bad luck on "Eke" day if chances on that day. Children born on Eke day are named Eke. I know of several Ibos whose last names are Eke. Well, if you ask any Mr. Eke to explain the meaning of Eke, they might endeavor to suit there purposes and say that Eke is a shortened variation of Ekejuba, which means the Creator has wealth. It may also be interpreted to mean that shared wealth is never satisfying. Eke could also mean Ekejiuba which could be interpreted to mean the Creator has wealth, as well depending on dialectics.

Eke is a man's name. Eke means Creator. Eke also means weekday. Eke is also a kind of big snake

A na m eke oke is a sentence that is interpreted to mean I am dividing something among people, just like you are dividing or splitting or sharing something among people or between people.

As to Eke the snake – it is the name of python or any of the large constricting snakes.

If an Ibo sees a big or large snake, he would describe it as though it is a python. As a matter of fact the feminine kind is guilty of this exaggeration in their attempt to describe what a monstrous snake they saw or encountered. There is as a result, a popular saying in Igbo language to indicate that every snake a woman sees is more often than not a python.

Agwo nwanyi huru na a bu Eke.

Agwo nwanyi huru na agho eke

The point again is to stress that one Igbo word may mean several things, depending on how that word is used in a sentence or sounded in speech.

Eke could be a shortened form of Okereke which is used to describe a child born on Eke day that has now grown into a man. Eke could also be a shortened form of Okeke courtesy of dialectic differences in the land.

Friday the thirteenth is also considered by some as a day of bad luck. This consideration has nothing to do with the Igbo culture but some try to be careful just as the West.

CHAPTER FIFTEEN

BUSINESS

Businesses in Igbo land are often family enterprises such as opening up of stalls, setting up shops and setting up manufacturing of wares, buying and retailing all sorts of articles of trade. Some businesses simply import what they sell from neighboring countries and overseas and are called importers. These importers are generically called traders and they hire apprentices who keep these stalls and shops for the owners. The shop-keepers do most of the retailing and are compensated at the end of their apprenticeship contract. Retailing of some of the imported materials are in home shops or ware-houses and wholesaling to smaller and petty traders are also practiced, enabling the importer to make a quick turn over of their wares to be able to raise liquidity for a return trip. Some businesses are family-run mostly by fathers who engage their children to help in after schools or during long vacations.

Family members are not usually paid wages or salaries because it is assumed that family members will benefit from family business. The children are expected by virtue of birth to the family to work for their fathers until they leave home for higher education. When this happens, it becomes the responsibility of the father to bear the child's cost of higher education from the proceeds of the family business. Most family businesses observe little accounting rules and principles. In fact, few keep records or try to keep a ledger or prepare accounting or income statements. Some sort of debtors' ledger may be kept just to record who buys things on credit, the amounts and the date they promise to pay for what they purchased. Cost of merchandise is recorded just to enable for the determination of selling price. Items sold on daily basis may be recorded by some but such books are not usually balanced for the purpose of presentation to auditors, internal or external.

Many family businesses do not prosper because they serve as piggy banks. Petty cash can range from a few hundreds to thousands, from lunch money to enough money to purchase vehicles for personal use. Most family businesses are run just like most households that rarely balance their checkbooks. In efforts to help extended family members and to help the society, most small and mid-sized merchandising businesses hire and employ relatives and extended family relations with absolute trusts. Large businesses are of a different situation altogether. Banks both local and those with international connections are run just like one can find in the United States of America and Europe.

Foreign exchanges and major foreign currencies are easily obtainable in Nigerian banks at Owerri, Okigwe, Orlu, Enugu, Aba, Umuahia, Awka, Onitsha as readily as in Lagos or Abuja. Foreign currencies are also easily exchanged in open markets, in stalls or in banks all over Igbo land.

PRICE BARGAINING

The biggest markets in Igbo are the Onitsha Market; the Aba Market; Ogbete Market and in many respects, the Afor Umuna Market in Okigwe. These are open markets with some stalls and lock-up shops. In these open markets, and they are common all over Southeastern Nigeria, bargaining for prices you want to pay for an item or article is expected. In department stores and supermarkets, prices are fixed by the retailer so bargaining is not allowed. When I say prices are fixed, it is to say that the price is already set on the product, and in most instances, written and pasted on the product for the prospective buyer to see. In some shops, if a customer buys many things and the retailer realizes huge profit, he may offer some discount in price, or give away some items free of charge, as goodwill.

When bargaining to sell an item, the seller starts by asking a very high price, while the buyer starts really low to make an offer on an item. This is like what one would observe at an auction except that the bargaining is between buyer and seller, and there are no fast-talking professionals involved here. To illustrate a typical price bargaining process, take a heap of yams for an example

Buyer:	How much are you selling this heap of yams?
Seller:	This particular heap is going for fifty dollar.
Buyer:	Would you accept twenty dollars for all of it?
Seller:	Twenty dollars for all these, no, that is too low.
Buyer:	What is the last price you would accept, and I mean the last price?
Seller:	I will let you carry the whole thing for thirty dollars, just because of you.
Buyer:	If you agree for twenty-two dollars, I will pay you cash right now.

Seller:	Well, you are my first customer today so, go ahead and pay me twenty-five, final price.
Buyer:	Thank you, and here is your twenty-five dollars.

This concludes a typical transaction in any open market in Igbo land. If this is a goat of sheep or rooster, the buyer examines every hole in the animal to make sure he gets his money's worth. If you are a stranger in an Igbo market place, you must delegate your purchases or ask a friend to tag along otherwise you will pay too much for any item or article of trade. You will definitely be taken advantage of if the seller realizes you are from far away land.

When you go to a supermarket, or drug store to fill a prescription, you are not to touch any item that you want to buy rather you tell the shopkeeper or the individual over the counter what you are looking to buy. The item will be picked up for you and you will be informed of the cost. If there are cheaper varieties of the same item, what could be considered generics, you will also be informed, and difference in quality and price explained to you also.

In a small corner shop, the store owner could also serve as the cashier, and will accept your money when purchase is decided upon. Purchases on credit are rare, unless you are someone familiar to the seller or a trusted customer to the establishment. Credit card are accepted at places that enjoy international flavor, but foreign currencies such as the US dollar, the Euro and the pound sterling are easily accepted.

SILENT TRADE - BARTERING YAMS

During the early eighteenth century, the Lander Brothers (European Explorer) were reported to have visited the Igbo Society to purchase yams. The largest market for yams they could find was in Igbo land, and the journey took them a minimum of ten days up the river to reach the market where they purchased these yams. In each situation, they succeeded in convincing the villagers to bring the yams down to their canoes at the banks of the Niger River.

EARLY TRADING CONTACTS WITH EUROPEANS

The Ibo who eventually traveled to the Gulf of Guinea with slaves met Europeans. They described Europeans as "strange-looking, pink-white dirty men, with pale un-kept beards." Because these Europeans wore shoes, the Ibo interpreted it that the men lacked toes so had to wear something (shoes) to help them walk and to maintain balance. Their noses were long, crooked and narrow and could get in the way if they wanted to drink from a cup. Ibo women believed that European women could melt in the sun if they took off their pith helmets.

The Ibo learned to distrust the Europeans and traders outside Igbo land because the Arabian and European goods were found to be defective. Their machetes and knives were of poor workmanship and easily broken, the inside of rolls of cloth with which these Europeans bought slaves were discovered to be rotten. They soon formed the opinion that foreigners were bad craftsmen, cheaters and liars.

Slave trade destroyed many defenseless people and made them objects of predatory raids, just to satisfy the demands for plantation labor in America. Native crafts and skills such as brass casting, ivory carving and cloth weaving were wiped out. The cost to West Africa was too great, considering that only the young and the healthy were enslaved, thus retarding the population.

Africans may have cooperated with European slave traders not out of love for man's inhumanity to man, but for other reasons which include the following:

1. Africans were forced into the slave trade initially by self defense. They were given guns, whisky, rum, and asked to choose between accepting these articles (which would enable them take slaves of their brothers and sisters) and risking being taken as slaves themselves.

2. Europeans forced African rulers to wage war with one another in order to take prisoners as slaves.

3. Europeans made slave trade so lucrative it became good business even for the interior inhabitants, that little thought was given to its depletive effect on the African human stock.

THE LACK OF RECORDED HISTORY

One of the reasons of lack of recorded history was the fact that Europeans confined their trading primarily along the coasts and had no opportunity to have seen first hand the interiors of Africa. States without direct access to the coasts traded through smaller coastal kings who thrived as middlemen in the growing trade between interior Africa and the ships of Europe. These kings maintained their monopoly by restricting Europeans to the sea.

When Lander brothers made their successful journey down the river Niger for instance, it was reported that their contacts with Ibos had been restricted to the "Ibos of the diaspora." These were the Igbo speaking people who settled far from their ancestral Igbo homelands or they could be non-Ibos who by their proximity and close association with the Ibos over the century made them Igbo-speaking. "Obi Ossai of Aboh presented himself as the king of the Ibos, and exercised what amounted to a monopoly of trade up and down the Niger valley."

SLAVE TRADE

For many centuries the Ibo used war captives as slaves, instead of killing them. These captive slaves were allotted farm lands and houses in Igbo land, but also required to work in their master's fields and homes. They were allowed to keep the produce from their own farms and profits they realized from selling what they produced. With these profits, a war captive could buy his freedom, and when this happens, the children become free men too. Most of these free men refuse to return to their homelands for fear they might be discriminated against, and their children not fully accepted. The Ibos soon forgot the ex-slaves' past and allowed them to enjoy equal status.

With the discovery of the new world in the 15th century, demand for cheap labor arose, and the Ibos started selling their war captives. They never realized the horrors awaiting these unfortunates in the hands of the slave traders. Ibos never saw the chains, the shackled captives, and the crowded hold of ships. Many of the slaves hoped for a better treatment in the hands of the Europeans than they had enjoyed in their old masters.

Initially, boat owners who approached the Ibos for their war captives paid them with cowries for every captive they delivered, man, woman, and child. Later, payments were made with guns, gunpowder, iron and copper utensils, tools and cloth. These transactions for years were done through middlemen, and the Ibos had no direct contact with the European slave traders.

THE OSU SYSTEM

Ibos make distinction between Diala and non-Diala in status system. Diala is a free-born citizen whose status at birth is symbolized by the burial of his umbilical cord, preferably at the foot of an oil palm tree. A Diala is free to attempt to gain title, and has no barrier to climbing social ladder in his community provided he can afford to foot the bill membership to these institutions demand.

In direct contrast, Ohu was a slave who had very few rights. Ohu has less stigma and is a lesser evil than Osu. Ohu eventually got absorbed into the lineage of the master they served, becoming their companions and in many situations marrying their daughters.

An Osu was a cult slave; a person who had been dedicated to a shrine or a deity and that person and his descendants are forever proscribed as social pariah or outcasts with no social rights which non-Osu are bound to respect. They were people hated and despised because they reminded the Diala of their guilt. The Osu were feared because they were protected by their deity from being sold or killed, and unlike the Ohu slaves, they could not be absorbed into their master's lineage.

Osu suffer social disability and are stigmatized from the point of view of marriage. It was a system of branding humans with a label of inferiority and of having descended from the strain of humans believed to be from the family of Osu or Ohu. The Osu system and its social stigma and label are as old and permanent as the soil of Igbo land.

The Osu system of slavery originated from the Owerri-Okigwe region of Southeastern Nigeria. The Diala belief is that the Osu are descended from a people who, at the recommendation a diviner, were dedicated to a deity, in order that they may become his servitor. A particular village lineage or individual that had been experiencing illness or misfortune would "dedicate" his slave to the deity, in the belief that the slave would then carry out the sins of the dedicator. This process is performed by walking the slave to the shrine, and making to sit down on the bare floor of the shrine facing the carved statues as he is being dedicated.

In 1956, in the Eastern House of Assembly, an attempt was made by Dr. Nnamdi Azikiwe through a bill, to abolish the Osu system and its allied practices, including the Ohu system. The recommendation of the Belonwu Bride Price Committee was that Osu system prevented certain people from being married by those who are descended from the best strain of the society. Dr Nnamdi Azikiwe merely argued on Humanitarian and altruistic grounds, equating the bill with Untouchability Act of India; the Magna Carta; the Abolition of Slavery; Emancipation Proclamation; and the Petition of Rights. Despite his efforts, fights, and good intentions, this social proscription and stigmatization of fellow human beings is still practiced as the tradition.

CALENDAR

The word Calendar is derived from the Latin Calendae, the first day of each month, when the appearance of the New Moon was solemnly proclaimed in ancient Rome. The moon and the sun once divided up the year in more even fashion. The year itself was solar and lasted for

365 days, the length of the annual course of the sun. But the months however related to the moon, and were based on the lunar and classic menstrual cycle of 28 days. Mathematically, if one divides the 365 day sun by one 28 day moon month, what we have is 13 months, the 13 lunar months, with one day over, giving us a year and a day, hence the leap year compensation every four years.(Diane Ferguson, - the magical year).

Ibos follow the same system for fixing the beginning, length and division of the year and arranging days in weeks and months in the same definite order as in the English calendar, with one minor exception. A Calendar week runs from Sunday through Saturday, but Monday being the beginning of the work week is considered the first day of the week in Igbo land. It has not been quite clear and no one has been able to say for sure if there was any legislation to the establishment of this fact, but I would say this is generally accepted and observed. As already mentioned above under market days, the Igbo recognizes one week as comprising of eight days.

"Izu Ukwu" means eight days (8 days)

"Izu Nta" means four days (4 days)

These tabular register of days in Igbo is based on market days, Afor, Nkwo, Eke, Orie. As a result, these eight days weeks are conventionally accepted and have been checked to correspond to the thirteen lunar months that represent the actual number of times the earth's natural satellite that shines by the sun's reflected light appears to us revolving about the earth from east to west in a year. Explaining this fact much may appear too scientific for our purpose here, but our fore fathers were that technical, even then. If an Ibo says "I will celebrate the birth of my son two weeks from next Afo market eve." You should count in terms of eight day weeks based on Afo, Nkwo, Eke and Orie. (Izu ukwu abuo) The New Yam festival lasted for a week

(Emume Iri Ji ohuru gara otu izu ukwu)

Also, the date of a particular day is written in a different order as we write here in the United States of America. First, the day, followed by the month and then the year. The measure of time goes from the smallest (the day) to the next in size (month) to the largest (the year).

Examples:

In Nigeria as a whole, December 5, 2005 is written thus: 05/12/2005

December 1, 2005 is written thus: 01/12/2005

This method of representing the time at which an event occurs might confuse an individual from the United States that has an engagement or an appointment with an Ibo business man to meet at a specified time.

DAY/ MONTH / YEAR BY NIGERIANS AND IN NIGERIA
MONTH /DAY/YEAR BY EVERYBODY IN AMERICA

Calendar days, time and dates will not present a problem for any foreigner or first time visitor to Nigeria or to any part of the Igbo land because you will be well advised to adjust your clock to local time and will also be made aware of how other countries write dates different from the Americans.

CHAPTER SIXTEEN

CELEBRATIONS

Celebrations come in several fashions, some cultural, some traditional while others are religious. These call for very elaborate and festive events. Ibos celebrate something for instance, birth of a child, naming ceremony, graduating from University on personal levels. National holidays are also celebrated, and some regional and local observances too. Some of these celebrations are held only for one day but some last for several days on end.

COMMUNITY

Ibos tend to associate with their kind and can be found all over the world. They very readily settle and form communities in any city where there are a few of them. Due to their social nature they easily make in-roads into positions of authority at the state and county levels including colleges and universities. Their sense of community, help them keep in touch with the less fortunate relatives anywhere. They strongly believe in the preservation of their cultural heritage and the importance of educating their children in the culture of their people, hence the essence of writing this book. Events like the New Yam Festival, ceremonies and religious practices are activities through which Ibos attempt to recreate and uphold the cultural rituals of the Igbo land.

COMPLEXION

Ibo people generally have light complexioned skin that could be described as chocolate brown. Some Western writers described Ibos as "mahogany-colored men from South East of the Niger River." Others described Ibos as "big-hearted and possess a desire of superiority, and make attempts to attain it, or excel in what is praiseworthy, without a desire of depressing others." One other author, Dryden described the Ibo in the following language: "A noble emulation beats their breasts". Literally, the Ibos are spoken of as the most imitative and emulative people in Africa. They are aggressive, frank, industrious and some may say, "arrogant", but introduce them to any manners and customs, they easily adapt themselves to them. Ibo traders were even referenced as red-men by the Europeans in the early 1800s. This was partly because characteristically, the men rubbed red liquid powder derived from cam wood on their body and into cloaks and other garments when approaching European traders. This was original and the earliest idea of today's military camouflage uniforms and outlook as soldiers prepare to go into ambush and stake-outs during military drills and mock battles.

Today, such practice of disguise and make-up effects are used in the United States, for instance by American type football players, movies like "Commando" and "Predator" in which Schwarzenegger Arnold may famous before becoming governor of California. Ibo traders lived in the Southeastern Nigeria mainly in villages. Today half of the youths and business people live in big cities and towns. The Ibos number more than thirty million, and live in extensive area. They speak Igbo and English, - English language spoken as a consequence of the British colonial domination of that territory of West Africa.

CONVENTIONALISM

There are basic good manners in the Igbo culture that must be observed, failure of which, could be considered rude and obnoxious. Attention is paid to conventional behaviors and established traditions, basic principles or procedures the Ibos have accepted as true or correct. When people do not know what to say in public, it is a time to be quiet, because Ibos believe that whatever one says will be attributed to him.

"Onu na enweghi ihe o kwuru ekwugbughi onwe ya."

Another Igbo popular adage says that "ukwu gaa ije laa, onu gaa o naghi a laa."

Literary translation - You can go anywhere on this planet and return home safely and without consequence, but whatever you say at any point, if significant, will never be forgotten or forgiven. This compares to the "Miranda rights" warnings that law enforcement agents are expected to read to citizens of the United States when they are about to be arrested. In the Igbo land, it is conventional wisdom not to pour out your heart or soul to complete strangers or volunteer information unless your life depends on it, otherwise be ready for the consequence.

Traditionally, Ibos believe and expect people to behave themselves properly in public places such as vacate a seat for an elderly person, in church, in buses, at social events and even at home. One should not put his feet up on a chair, table or desk, but if one happened to have lost his manners and gets carried away and commits these infractions, the moment a senior or an elderly walks in, he removes his feet and dusts off the chair or desk. People do not sit on tables even in the privacy of their own homes. You are not expected to leave your hands in your pockets while holding a conversation with an equal, nor is it proper to leave one hand in your pocket while you greet or shake someone's hand. You may not leave your hands in your pants pockets when you are talking to your senior or being spoken to by a senior person, and especially teacher or parent. You may not walk away or smile when a teacher, a parent or your senior is addressing you. Children do not talk back at their parents or teachers for any reason at any age. Holding a conversation is another way of saying that you are engaged in a conversation with someone.

Mourning conventions are strong in Igbo land and must be strictly observed for instance, the dress code of the survivor of either spouse is black. If a husband dies, the surviving wife or wives must shave clean their hair/heads in paying due respect, and must wear black clothes for a period of twelve months. The same is expected of the man that loses his wife. Absolutely, the grievingpartner must not have sexual intercourse during a mourning period, except where a man married more than one wife, and loses one of the wives and the living still functioning wife demands it.

If a father dies, all the unmarried children will shave their heads, but not the married children. They will all grieve the same but the married daughters may pin up black patch cloth on their clothes just above their breast pocket on left side of their chests.

COMPLIMENTS

The Ibos do not take compliments too seriously, except for the feminine kind who wants to hear it regularly, lest they feel unloved. Formal and respectful recognition or the expression of high esteem, respect, affection and admiration are not rare among the Ibos. However, if someone compliments you, pretend as though you do not deserve the compliment, otherwise you will be considered arrogant and full of yourself. The appropriate response would be to blush and dismiss the compliment ever so politely. If the individual reinforces his observation, or admiring remark you must acknowledge the individual and tell him how appreciative you are of his kind recognition.

Examples of compliments and most probable responses:

"You are looking good"
"You are dressed to kill"
"What is the occasion?"
"You have a beautiful/lovely family"
"Gini ka mmadu ga eme?"
"E nwere onye o bu ike aka ya?"
"O nweghi onye o bu ike aka ya!
It is not completely of my making or a greater power should
  have all the credit.

"You are trying a lot"
"E n'agbali kwa nke ukwu"

"ihe n'ile bu ike Chukwu"
"we put all things in God's hands"

 Ka anyi kele Chukwu
Anyi kelere Chukwu

We thank God

CONVERSATION

Conversation between Ibos are always held at low voices almost to the point of whisper, but mostly very fast and punctuated with many gestures. There is almost never a lack of oral exchange of sentiments, observations, opinions or ideas when Ibos meet. Any topic can stimulateconversation ranging from office gossip, the opposite sex, politics, current affairs to world events. When Ibos raise their voices, it is always misconstrued as aggressive behavior, in anger and for the most part disrespectful. Under normal circumstances raising one's voice prompts the listener to caution you not to raise your voice on him and if the caution is not heeded, quarrel will result even at a point where a fight ensues. More than one person can talk at one time but not necessarily at one another. This is a way the Ibo signals that he would speak next or that you have spoken for more than the expected length of time or to imply that he too has an important point or some contribution to make on the issue that is being discussed. People may start to talk before a preceding speaker finishes. In conversation or informal conversation, animated or not, this is not considered rude or disrespectful. In fact, at times, someone's failure to interrupt could be taken or considered a sign of the person's lack of interest in the speaker or what is being said.

CHAPTER SEVENTEEN

CULTURE

Ibos have a set of shared attitudes, values, goals and practices among them which place great deal of emphasis on self-reliance, equality, democracy, and strong competition for social, economic and political progression to higher stages of development. The Igbo ethnic group is among the largest peoples of Nigeria, and they live at the crossroads of cultures. It is not very uncommon to find a family where all the children go to church every Sunday, whose parents are chief priests to idol worshipers. The children may grow up as religious people even when their parents refuse to give up their heathen ways of worship. I remember growing up in Okai village in Umuna town of Okigwe as a good Christian and regular church member. I was baptized before my first birthday and I received all the sacraments of the Catholic faith before puberty. Everything about religion I learned at school because my parents believed in the ancestral ways of saying praises to God, which the missionaries told the young minds were idol worship and non-religious. Some cultural activities like the New Yam Festival is being frowned at by the "holier than thou" Christians because festivities of the sort mention Yam, and not communion. These amount to mere misconceptions people front in isolated cases when they lack reasons to celebrate Igbo culture.

I remember inviting a few of my family friends in Northern California to the Okigwe Family Union of Northern California (OFUNC) culture day, an organization I was privileged to chair for three years, the annual New Yam Festival that takes place during mid-August, and the reply I got in 2005, was that they are Christians and attending such festivity would amount to worshiping yam, since in the program, there are two items calling for yam and kola presentation, respectively. One of the families hails from Mbano, Okigwe and the other, from Ondo State.

A similar situation, at a symposium on Ozo title system in Enugu in 1977, Uchendu stated that he was mildly surprised when a delegate from one of the states in northern Nigeria argued that "Religion is not part of Culture" (Uchendu, 1988: 17-18) He responded by saying that "Religion is nothing if not an essential part of culture, what makes aspect of religion so emotionally contentious is that they are eminently cultural, whatever other elements society and managers of religious organizations attribute to them" , he concluded.

Clyde Kluckholn (1963: 24) "to be human is to be cultured", Believing that "anthropology holds up a great mirror to man and lets him look at himself in his infinite variety" (Kluckholn) 1963: 19, 24, 28-34. He goes on to define culture as that part of the environment that is the creation of man; a way of thinking, feeling, a theory that helps us to understand a mass of otherwise chaotic (social) facts; a store house of pooled learning of the group found in the memories of old man and woman, in books and material objects created by man; and the learned experiences by individuals as the result of belonging to some particular group. Cultures produce needs as well as provide a means of fulfilling them; every culture is a precipitate of history; culture throws up to history social facts which the sieve of history can hold, in changed or unchanged form, but always with altered meanings. Culture is also defined as a map, an abstract but approximate representation of a particular cultural entity enabling the young and stranger to find their way into particular cultures as bearers, creators, consumers, and products of culture (Ahiajoku lecture Series: 1988).

I could not agree more or have expressed my leanings more eloquently than these academicians.

The masquerade is another aspect of the Igbo culture that seem to clash with religious interests of a few professing Christians. Mask carving is the central being of our culture the focal point where all other aspects of the Igbo culture appear to converge, so deserve further study and research for posterity. There was one instance that polarized an entire town in present day Onuimo Local Government Area of Okigwe, Imo State for years when religious beliefs and misinterpretations resulted in dire consequences. The building of a community library came to a complete halt, and a prospective priest was denied ordination after completing fifteen years of Catholic Seminary education because he was the son of a major player in one of the two camps. The prospective priest was the son of the leader of one faction of the town who strongly believed that religion and culture can both co-exist. The other faction that believed that all Christians should denounce all aspects of the Igbo cultural festivities petitioned the catholic bishop at the diocese headquarters and protested that the town's son should not be ordained a priest due to his father's position. This ordination was delayed for twenty years.

LEFT - HANDED PEOPLE

Left-handedness is looked at as a fault or disability and considered wrong in the Igbo culture. Exhibiting left-handedness attracts attention in a negative way and considered abnormality. Early in life if a parent observes that his child is showing a definitive tendency toward becoming left-handed it becomes a family decision as to how that could be discouraged promptly. One of the options would be to let the child wear heavy wrist bands on the left hand, making it awfully difficult for the left hand to be moved with ease, let alone perform with. An extreme option would be to inflict a serious open wound on purpose that would require bandaging and long period of time to heal. Generally the child would favor the use of his right hand because the left hand has been put out of use. By the time the left hand heals, the child will be accustomed to using the right hand for all the right reasons. This would be considered "child cruelty or abuse" in the United States. The child is discouraged from using the left hand more frequently than the right hand before the wound heals completely. As the child nurses the wound on the left hand, he learns to depend more on the use of the desired hand, the right hand, and in the process, out-grows his dependency on the use of the left hand. Left-handed people are said to walk the wrong way, do things left-handedly, lack dexterity and are very clumsy.

The cultural belief of the Ibos is that the right thing to do is to use the right hand in doing things and the left hand as a support or to assist the right.. If an Ibo man gives you something, you must accept it with the right hand. If you stretch out your left hand to accept something from an Ibo man your gesture is considered offensive and insulting. Such behavior is considered very disrespectful, lacking of good manners and indicative of not being able to appreciate what is offered or who gives it.

If you are invited to dinner in a private home you do not stick your left hand in the food of dish, otherwise you will be considered as have insulted or disrespected the people at the table. The Ibos at the table will look at one another in awe, and would wonder what planet you hail from that you lack the most basic manner at table in Igbo land.

On extreme situations those who adhere to the practices of the Igbo tradition could very readily abandon the table and the entire meal in disgust, all because you were eating with the wrong hand. A few of the names used to describe left-handedness in Igbo language are.

Aka ekpe

Aka eda

Aka ruru aru

In the United States of America, being left-handed is considered a gift. In baseball, an America game, a pitcher who is left-handed is paid very high premium, and is highly sought after. A left-handed pugilist is considered to be more problematic for his opponent than a right-handed one, and as a result considered odds on favorite.

My favorite America president, not that he did anything for me, William Jefferson Clinton is left-handed, and is President George Bush Sr. and Ronald Reagan too. Some talking heads on television claim that left-handed people are more intelligent and more organized. One Dr. Oz, who appeared on one of the talk show circles, the Oprah Show, in May of 2007, tried to substantiate such claims. Oprah Winfrey was happy to hear everything and anything good about left-handed people, one guest she had whose name was Dr. Oz had to say to her and her audience of course, you guessed it, Oprah Winfrey could also left-handed.

CHAPTER EIGHTEEN

COURTSHIP AND MARRIAGE

Igbo marriage custom helped widen the sense of community by encouraging men to take wives from outside their own lineage. The marriage relationships also encouraged multiple contacts that forged links stretching across several villages, leading to inter-village trading When disputes erupted between villages, relationships through marriage formed a basis for organizing mutual defense, thereby modifying the severity of warfare between villages. Although things are changing, traditional customs that differ from those of the Igbo culture still exist. Group co-educational activities begin quite early, at about fourteen. Major forms of entertainment are attending dances, choir practices, sporting events, moonlight nights, etc. Dating is a much restricted and individualized thing without connotations. Pairing off is done only when marriage is completed.

Few dating ever result in marriage even today, because the males marry in their late twenties and early thirties, while the females marry in their early or late twenties. The men indulged in a plurality though seldom in more than two, but they did not however, preserve the same constancy to their wives that they expected from them. Both parties were betrothed when young by their parents, but some males have been known to betroth themselves, and especially in modern times.

It is customary in Igbo land for a man to ask a woman's hand in marriage through the father of the woman. Parents and relatives of either party exert very strong influence in the acceptance or rejection of a prospective marriage or marriage proposal, because the new comer to the family becomes a member of an extended family system. Long drawn-out engagements are rare, and are usually scorned as a sign that the young man does not have the resources yet and had better remained a bachelor than clamping on a young lady that would have been snapped off the market a long time ago. Young men who do not aspire to higher standards of living than their fore-fathers tend to marry early and settle down to raise own families, and are attracted to females of like goals and aspirations, and may possess little education, usually below high school education. Those who aspire to pursue higher education tend to postpone or defer marriage, and depending on the level of education.

A civil (traditional) ceremony is necessary for the marriage to be legally accepted and approved. Religious ceremony may add to the recognition, but must have to follow later. Newly weds must as a custom move away from the family of the groom and for this reason alone, the Ibo man does not take a wife until he is ready and have established himself well enough to be the head of a family.

Another reason is that the young bride will not have much freedom to establish her domain, walk around her husband without restriction or intimidation, make demands that are obvious or even outrageous, now that her attributes are intact and worthy of private showing. The young couple will however live within the compound of the groom's father but in a new house which family members help build.

MARRIAGE

Marriage on itself is very important to the Ibo people of Nigeria. The practice of marriage in Ibo culture is viewed as "the core of the whole social structure" because, "until a person is married, he or she is not regarded as a distinct individual" This belief is said to have tied family to "religious definition of adult existence," since individuals from time the of marriage, take it upon themselves to care for a new family. Prior to the European influence traditionally, preparation for marriage began in childhood and was concluded on the wedding day. The maturation of females began at the age of seven years old when, in preparation she is taught simple domestic tasks such as housekeeping and farm work. At the time of her first menstrual cycle she is instantly ready for proposal, and her parents will keep her in seclusion for eight days. Nature has proclaimed her a woman, and her hand could be asked in marriage.

Marriage proposal by a prospective groom begins with a ritual known as ibu mmanyi ajuju, where the young man officially asks permission to marry the girl. This also permits for questions on family background to be raised to prevent forbidden marriages, that may result, for instance, of incest, ohu, osu or ume. If the girl's parents agree to the marriage the prospective groom will then authorize the numerous stages of marriage rituals to commence, uninterrupted. Marriage in Ibo culture concludes with the payment of dowry or bride price to the bride's family, considered the endowment or fee for marriage contract.

The marriage institution is an important part of the Igbo life and culture. Until the Catholic Christian religion introduced celibacy as a virtue, an unmarried Igbo male cuts a sad picture of hopeless poverty; and unmarried female was a social disaster. Our ancestors in their wisdom provided us cultural alternatives in the form of polygamy and concubinage which give every adult access to a spouse or consort. (Uchendu; 1965:187-97).

Every big event in Igbo land is celebrated with dances, songs and music that particularly depict the event. There have been a few informalities in the details lately, and varies from communities to communities in different parts of the Igbo land. In the written Igbo language below a few of the names around the family or in dating, but before that, a brief discussion on customary wedding

WEDDING

The wedding itself in many parts of the Igbo land can be quite a gay affair. On the occasion a feast is prepared, and the bride and bridegroom stand up in the midst of all their friends and well-wishers, who are assembled for this purpose, as he declares that she is thenceforth to be looked upon as his wife, and no person is to pay an address to her. This is thus proclaimed in the vicinity on which time the bride retires from the assembly. After she is brought home to her husband, another feast is made, to which the relations of both parties are invited. Her parents then deliver her to bridegroom, accompanied with a number of blessings.

In some parts of the land, at the same time, they tie around her waist a cotton string of the thickness of the goose quill, which none buy only married women are permitted to wear. She is now considered as completely his wife. To enable the married couple start making a living, they are given gifts such as a piece or portion of land, domestic animals such as goat, sheep, and dog; household goods and implements of husbandry. Gifts come from friends of both parties, after which the ceremony is considered ended. Festival is celebrated with music, dancing and loud acclamation of joy and lots of food to eat.

ENGLISH	IGBO
Man	Nwoke
Woman	Nwanyi
Father	Nna
Mother	Nne
Boy	Okorobia
Girl	Agbo-gho
Inlaw	Ogo (or-gor)

Brother	Nwanna or (Nwanne nwoke)
Siste	Nwanne nwanyi
Husband	Di (Dee)
Wife	Nwu-nye
Chieftain	Nze; Ozo
King/Queen	Eze
Old man	Agadi nwoke
Old woman	Agadi nwayi or Ibiri-achi

GENDER ROLES IN IBO CULTURE

The male in Igbo land is an institution because to be a male carries with it the aura of spirituality beyond masculinity. Men are the head of the family or household, while women are considered part of the man. Only the men perform rituals during cultural festivities and traditional events. The traditional role of women in Igbo society has been subordinate, men paying a bride prize for their wives in the form of dowry. This tradition has not denied Ibo females the right to attain socioeconomic status in their own rights, especially in modern times, due to European influence. Ibo women are considered very powerful on sexual level, based on traditional view of sexual desire as potentially dangerous and the acknowledgement of female ability to sexually manipulate

The term "division of labor and specialization" feature so prominently in gender roles of traditional Igbo society than in economics. Men are the bread winners or the providers of the family, as well as the protectors. The men are expected to work outside of the home, and pay the bills while the women clean, cook, and look after and nurse the children when the man is away in the farm. Men perform such tasks as maintenance, harvesting of crops, lead the community, and sit on committees settling disputes. Both parents can discipline their children but major issues are deferred till the man comes home, and children try really hard to avoid situations getting to that.

In politics, women can only participate in an all-female council and other political structures that parallel their male counterparts. These female components are less powerful because a female is rarely elected to wield power over men.

Chastity was important value in traditional Igbo society until the European influence. A female is never to have known a man before marriage, and must remain a virgin till the wedding night. Fertility and child-rearing are the pride and essence of marriage, and not necessarily romance or love, although these two components develop in the process of successful marriage. Women are honored and admired profoundly and respectfully when pregnant or after giving birth, especially to sons.

Women are blamed when they are unable to give birth to a son and in extreme situations, a man could take a second wife just because the wife was unable to give him a son.

A woman can leave her husband if the husband is impotent. In fact, sexual impotency of the man or a wife's dissatisfaction with her husband's sexual performance can lead to divorce because emphasis is placed on male sexual prowess in Igbo culture. In traditional society it is acceptable for a young wife to take lovers or have extramarital relationships when a man is incapable due to major accident or premature death of a young man, if the wife decides to stay in the marriage.

POLYGAMY/BIGAMY

Polygamy, the marriage in which a man may have more than one wife at the same time is necessitated by numerous factors in Igbo culture. Bigamy on the other hand is the act of entering into a marriage with one person while still legally married to another. The misconception in the West has been that Africans marry several wives at the same time, and little is done on their part to find out why. They wrongly envision polygamy as a definite sign of sexual promiscuity. A man's economic standing may endow him the privilege of marrying more than one wife at a time and also as a cultural alternative to celibacy. The decision to take a second wife oftentimes enjoys the whole-hearted support of the first wife. In fact, there are instances where the first wife has taken the initiative in recommending some other female she would rather share her husband with. If the second wife too is unable to bear fruits, there could be a possibility that a third wife is contemplated and so on, until the family is blessed with children. Some wives welcome the addition of new wives to the household because it eases their domestic load. Besides, women age very early and lose their attraction for men.

Another scenario that prompts an Ibo man to marry a second wife is the failure of the first wife to have a son. Girls are not considered as good as boys in terms of children who would represent and carry on the family torch forever, because they soon get married and are taken away by their husbands. They drop and lose the family names and in the absence of a male child, the family name stays lost. The Ibo man wants this dilemma avoided during his lifetime if humanly possible, and because Ibos place great value in posterity.

The other circumstance that led an Igbo man to marry a second wife in the past was the need for farm hands. Farming was the main occupation on rudimentary scale, and basically all food was locally grown. The staple foods of the Ibos were yam and cassava. Yam, the main crop is planted between the months of February and May. Yam planting season starts when the Ibo sees the first rainfalls of the year for early planters. The family, mostly the males, young and old alike till the soil and build mounds in which to place the yam seedlings. Ibo's livelihood came from working the land, and because cultivating the soil required intense labor, no single person can do it alone, successfully. To be successful at any scale, one has to hire laborers as extra hands and pay them by selling part of previous year's harvest. If planning for the long run, a long range plan would be to take as many wives as you can manage so they can help you in the farms. A few years down the road, the marriage to the numerous wives could be blessed with children, and you and your wives will have more help in the farm, as you and your wives get old –the love for many children.

Disputes over pieces of land and cash crops between individuals could also prompt an Ibo man to marry more than one wife. Most conflicts were settled when families were out-numbered or physically over-powered. A man and his one –wife family could be beaten up by a large family because during the olden days, the court system was virtually non-existent. Might was right, and peoples' fertile lands were easily wrestled from them by the strong, out of envy or the knowledge that such person has no lineage. If a family is not out-manned, they are able to at least put up a fight, or die trying to protect what is rightfully yours or that which must remain in the family.

Other reasons for polygamy include but not limited to men wanting to refrain from intercourse with a woman pregnant or nursing a baby. Many men like change especially if a man discovers that his wife is taking her hygienic upkeep for granted.

NWANYI NO NA EZI

During the readjustment of the uterus at monthly intervals that result in discharge of blood, secretions, and tissue debris in non-pregnant female breeding-age primates (dictionary definition), women are considered to be in their nature's most unclean state and traditionally are avoided.

Many years ago, every woman in Igbo culture was forbidden at that certain times of the month to come into a man's dwelling house, or to touch any person or any thing we eat. Ono na ezi means she is outside, and will stay out until purified. If a child is so fond of the mother that he touches or cannot avoid touching her at this period, he suffers the consequence of which he was obliged to be kept out and sentenced to the little house with his mother until purification offering is made.

CHAPTER NINETEEN

DEMOCRACY

Democracy first existed in Igbo land before Europeans arrived there. Every form of government known today in Europe and America first existed in Africa centuries before the Europeans arrived. Government of the people for the people by the people is the old definition of democracy.

Try defining democracy in the United States of America and you will be amazed at what interpretations the average American will offer you. Some have democracy to mean freedom. Others mistake democracy to mean presidential system of government or a republic.

Early Europeans to arrive in West Africa found out first hand that Ibos differ from other West African ethnic groups in quite a number of ways. Firstly, they discovered that Igbo communities were not monarchies. They discovered that the Ibos had a system in which everyone has a say, and reserved the right to be heard until a consensus of opinion was reached. This art of governing the Europeans admired the most, copied, exported to their homelands and struggled with till they were able to convince their imperial monarchies to allow their subordinates to be heard. This is the year, two thousand and seven, so imagine how Queen Isabella of Spain would have reacted, or the British Monarch, the French, the German or the Emperor of Rome to such suggestions a hundred years ago. The Europeans were amazed that the Ibo people were knit together spiritually, and governed loosely by councils of elders. They also observed a system of representation and a balloting of age groups.

The villages were bound together into clans of inhabitants that descended from a common ancestor. Cultural groups as a result were and still are made up of perhaps a hundred clans, all speaking the same dialect. The council of elders and the village assembly were the two political institutions that set up the Igbo system of government which today is known as democratic form of government. The village assembly strengthened popular participation and advocated that decisions must be taken only when unanimous, thereby ensuring governance by consent of the governed. The judicial system also encouraged popular involvement, and a pattern of government that nourishes broad uniformity in arbitrating quarrels by elders and more serious disputes and crimes by the council of elders and the village assembly.

The most popular and elaborate assembly has always been the village market. It still remains the focal point of social and economic activity of the Igbo life, because most arrangements and organizing of social life of the village and surrounding areas are made there. In addition to the considerable economic activities taking place at the village markets, the affairs of the clans are discussed and settled there.

Nigeria is a republic that boasts presidential system of governance but voting and elections are not almost fair and legitimate. Dishonesty is quite documented at almost every level of elective office from local to the presidential. It is not always the most qualified or the most deservedly elected individual that gets the nod to elective office. Money buys everything including friendship, power, popularity and influential positions of authority and leadership. When they get into positions of power, selfish aims and personal enrichment crop up as priorities.

CHAPTER TWENTY

DISCUSSIONS

Formal treatment of any topic or consideration of a question on culture, a situation that calls for an open debate or common sense and knowledge of the Igbo language should dictate the suitability of intervening in a discussion of certain issues. Issues and topics such as religion, politics and world affairs are important to the Igbo man and should be handled with care. Politics especially is a very important common topic of conversation, and can be very heated at times.

DRESS CODE

Igbo culture places great emphasis on appearance and therefore on jewelry. As a matter of fact, African jewelry has been given tremendous attention for centuries, because of their uniqueness and symbolic values. The chieftains and titled men make very powerful statements as they adorn these elegant and memorable jewelry. The women appear and look not only expensive but also beautiful. Ibos of all ages usually give importance to what they wear. On social gathering situations they place high premium on their appearance. The appropriateness and look of the particular clothing outfit is considered preponderant. Cost may not be a primary object of concern when choosing ceremonial outfits. Ibos like casual dressing such as jeans clothing on sneakers but they do not consider the outfits appropriate as white-collar work clothes during weekdays at major offices. Trousers and dress shirts are the norm, along with dress shoes. To make good impression in business circle one has to dress impeccably and in shirt and neckties, business suits or coats. A well-dressed Ibo man who is a professional likes a perfect fit of polished image that would express very personal style. There is this belief in the relationship between how he dresses and his success thus would strive to look his best. When dressing casually, top quality clothes that go together are usually considered. Even the non-professional makes dressing well a powerful tool in influencing locals at church services and social outings.

Sunday service clothes are more formal for both sexes, but the females never enter a place of worship without properly covering their hair and make-ups were not allowed. I use the word were to indicate how far the catholic church has changed today from what it used to be in the sixties and seventies. While the Western influence in clothing and manner of dressing up are manifest in the appearance of the Ibos, they have regional costumes and quite colorful and elaborate regalia that are worn at different occasions and festivities. There are chieftain regalia coronation attire and seasonal wears. Ibos dress in very uncomplicated ways because the temperature of the area is warm for most of the year. In the olden days loin cloths were worn while working in the family farms and these are times when the heat of the sun's rays are very intense. These were cloths that covered a man's manhood as he concentrates on his farm work. The outfits looked like a typical Japanese sumo wrestler's outfit that you see on television today. These were wide cotton scarves that were long enough to go around an average man's waist between the thighs, under and wrapped cleanly and coming up the wrap around with a flap of about one foot long covering the front and back of the bottom. Some of these scarves were wide and long and prevented any wardrobe type malfunction throughout the day's physical activities. These scarves were hand-woven with decorative plaited ends, expensive, elegant and are works of art to tie and depict maturation. It may not have made any sense to the early Europeans who saw the Ibo man from a distance misconstrued and generalized that the African had tail. Who knows what early Europeans would have said about a Sumo wrestler climbing a palm tree to tap palm wine in his outfits at the prime of civilization or when the explorers first saw non-Europeans.

Short pants are also worn that cover the hips and thighs fitting snugly at the lower edges near the knee. Depending on the nature of farm work one is doing, straw-hats may be worn, provided they won't interfere with work. After work, a man dresses up by changing into nicer clothes which cover him from the hips to the knees. He may put on a cape or cotton shirt of colorful local fabric.

When capes are worn, they are long and tied over the shoulder and under the right arm. The right arm is conventionally kept free. A titled man is a very important person and wears a red cap decorated with a leather band around it that holds eagle's feathers. He also wears gold anklets, and with his goatskin bag on his left shoulder he holds his specter or staff or an expensive eagle feather fan in his right hand. The fan serves two very important functions, to indicate a man's role in the town or village and to cool him down at every stroke of its wave in the air. Today, Ibos like many other African cultures wear Western clothes and dress attires, some types of unique traditional outfits are making noticeable comebacks.

The difficult thing today is that Ibos are indistinguishable from the Yoruba or the Hausa when they put on traditional wears, in any real sense of the word tradition. The long loose gown costumes of the Yoruba tunic with dagi knot and the Islamic motif of the Hausa or more appropriately, Northern Nigerians are equally worn by Ibos. Younger people dress more informally unless it is an occasion that calls for some more elaborate fanciful clothing or outfit.

Little boys wear loose type shirts, while little girls wear long flowing gowns or dresses. As boys get older, they wear shorts and girls may tie wrapper cloths on the lower half of their dresses or gowns. Married women wear cotton blouses and wrapper cloths that cover them from shoulder to their ankles. They adorn jewelry especially bracelets to show riches and how generous their husbands can be, when on social outings or at festivities. Showy clothes and attires are worn at rituals or on special occasions.

Other clothes may be worn for modesty, position or status in the village or town or as a display of wealth or simply to protect one from weather conditions. There is a popular Igbo adage that typifies this feeling. "The beauty of a woman is a measure of her husband's wealth"

"Mma nwanyi by di."

CHAPTER TWENTY-ONE

FARMING

Nigerian cash crops –groundnuts, cocoa, and palm produce are cultivated alongside food plants, although the latter largely remained on a subsistence basis, and therefore export trades served largely to supply many rural Nigerians with some cash. Kola nuts and palm oil for instance, were sent to the north, which in turn sent cattle to the south.

CLUSTERS OF FRESHLY HARVESTED OIL PALM NUTS
Photo by: Naturallycurly.com

The oil palm nuts are extracted for its oil and kernels for numerous uses; such as soap making, butter, food ingredient and preparation, local candles, moisturizers and ointment. The oil is also a major export product of the Ibos of Southeastern Nigeria.

PALM OIL

When slavery was abolished, palm oil was found and it became the only legitimate or legal trade left. Slave traders along the River Niger delta used their talents to build trade in the Igbo palm oil areas of Eastern Nigeria. This trade became so valuable that the British government appointed John Beecroft as consul. Palm oil could easily be prepared by boiling the husks in water, skimming off the oil, and selling it to the traders who traveled to the markets. African merchants bought the oil from the people, took it to the oil ports in the Niger delta or to

Lagos, and there sold it to the British representing firms in Liverpool. Palm oil from the Igbo land was found to produce the best and richest lather in soaps, and to be suitable for lubrication. Gradually, those who have been dependent on the slave trade turned to the collection and sale of palm oil. The palm oil trade grew, extending that form of trade relationships between African and European merchants. Before the year 1914, Germany had imported 44 percent of Nigerian exports, mainly palm oil; the war cut their trade and transferred the palm oil monopoly to the British merchants.

VILLAGE GIRL CRACKING OIL PALM KERNELS
Photo: Peacecorps.mtu.edu

Ibos crack their own palm-kernels. Palm kernels are cracked to separate the kernels to be sold in the local markets. Cracking palm kernels for your mother is a major chore in the villages. Mothers count on their children to crack enough for them when assigned to do so before the market day, because it is a major source of income for the house wives and women. In "Things Fall Apart" Chinue Achebe wrote: "Those whose palm kernels are cracked for them by a benevolent spirit should learn to be humble." If one is well-endowed which means born with "silver spoon" in one's mouth, his palm kernels have already been cracked for him prior to birth.

Achebe may have had something else in mind or may have a different interpretation when he wrote his famous book, but as the Ibos say, "Ilu bu uka, uka bu ilu."

CRACKED OIL PALM KERNELS

CASSAVA

Cassava is a perennial shrub with edible roots. It flourishes in Igbo land, and it is also grown in other tropical and subtropical areas of the world. It is a staple food, and a basis of many products.

The most common uses in Igbo land are as food for human consumption, starch, and animal feed. It provides the basic daily source of dietary energy. Cassava roots are processed into a wide variety of granules, flours, pastes or consumed freshly boiled, raw, grits, fermented, or pounded. The leaves are also consumed as a green vegetable which provides protein and vitamins A and B. Domesticated animals like goat, sheep, pig, cow also feed on the leaves in the farms or as fodder. It is used as a substitution for wheat flour. It can be made into foufou, akara, gari, salad, pudding and tapioca.

YAM

Yam is the king of crops in Igbo land. For years, it was a measure of wealth in the Igbo community. It is a very important crop in almost all of West Africa, but in Igbo land, only men cultivate yams, and build yam barns. The harvest of yam in Igbo land marks the beginning of the New Year, and the beginning of a season of plenty. Yam is a sacred symbol around which centers the Igbo religious life. Its sanctity is manifested in the belief that yam should not be stolen either from the farm or while still in the ground or in the barn. It is the "Ahianjoku" and people swear by it as a deity. Such an offense is believed to be punishable by death.

LARGE YAM BARN – INDICATIVE
OF WEALTHY IBO FARMER

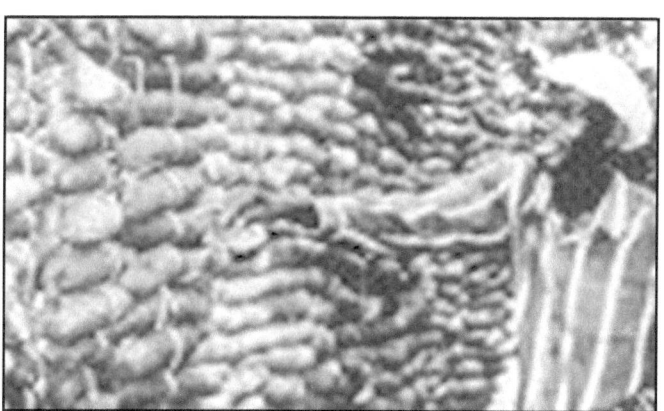

YAM BARN IN NIGERIA
World Bank Photo

CHAPTER TWENTY-TWO

FAMILY AND FRIENDS

Family is a term used loosely in Igbo land and culture. It is used to include extended family members. The extended family is considered as a very important social unit in Igbo culture and includes the father, mother, children, spouses, grandchildren, cousins, grandparents, aunts and uncles. Family members may have some internal problems, but when outside the family they will protect and fight for one another. This is so because family ties are very strong in the Igbo culture. Ibos very readily welcome family members into their homes and social events, even those family members they have never heard of before seeing them. All that is necessary is for some stranger to introduce himself as a relative of some distant cousin and he is readily welcomed into the family circle. This may seem minor a concept but it is esteemed important enough to be elevated into a proverb that commands general acceptance in Igbo culture.

Ihe a na ezi mmadu ezi bu nwa nne ya.

What you can always show someone is a new brother or sister or family relation that exists elsewhere. Ibos believe you cannot show someone his new friend, because people make their own friends. Family is very important in Igbo culture and that is why when an Ibo travels to a new city, state or country, he seeks out a relation or friend of a relation to stay with till he becomes familiar with the area and finds himself, or is able to fend for himself. If an Ibo travels to a town or city for a short stay, he seeks a family member, relative or friend of a family member rather than checking in and out of hotels or motels. In a situation where one family is rich or famous in an entire town, everyone from that town will use the one individual family to serve as a form of reference for lineage or credit and personal reference in social functions. Take for instance the Okoroike family. Very many people will claim to know the Okoroike family of Umuna Okigwe, Nigeria, or somehow related to them.

A bu m nwanne ndi ulo Okoroike, ndi nke umu ha guru oke akwukwo n'ala America, bikwa na obodo America.

I am related to the Okoroike family whose sons were educated in the United States of America, who also live in America.

A bu m nwanna Okoroike nke nwere ego nke ukwuu.

I am related to the Okoroike family the rich folks of Onuimo Local Government Area of Imo State, Nigeria.

A bu m nwanna Okoroike ndi nke nwere ego, chiri echichi, am ha putara ihe ma gi gawa Owerri.

I am related to the rich Okoroike family the titled chieftains whose compounds are the envy of the town, this side of the Imo River , if you are going to Owerri.

With young people leaving home for the big cities and even to Europe and the Americas, the nuclear family is a growing and observable fact, even in the face of changing economic and social conditions. The word "Friend" is used literally in Igbo language. The Ibo man will address someone as friend if he does not know that individual by name. Friend means Enyi

Onye mmadu a maghi ka o na akpo enyi ya.
Girl friend enyi nwanyi
Boy friend enyi nwoke

These are terms used by the opposite sex
Oyi nwanyi girl friend
Oyi nwoke boy friend
Enyi m nwoke   my boy friend
Enyi m nwanyi   my girl friend

Again, it must be emphasized here that the above terms are strictly used by the opposite sexes.

Friend is appropriately used to address or describe a classmate -- "Ezigbo Enyi"

In Igbo context and culture a real friend is difficult to define. He has to be someone you can trust. This individual must know all your secrets and may use them against you. In other words, a good friend may turn out to be your worst enemy, because he knows all your secrets. So, Ibos rarely confide in friends, except where the bond is strong, and even in such instances, there are certain things you would rather not divulge to a friend.

Iro ka nsi   Hatred is worse than poison

Enyi a laa la   Friendship is out of the door

When a foreigner hears the saying "It takes a village to raise a child", they misinterpret the adage in different directions. This is not about universal health coverage or the "no child left behind" catch phrase one hears during presidential primaries in the United States of America. It means that when an Ibo sees a child stray or do something wrong, he does not wait for the natural parent to give permission for correction. You point the child in the correct direction just as you would do to your own blood. "Spare the rod and spoil the child" is a similar maxim if you will. The cultural difference is that spanking or padding a child for justifiable reason is permissible in Igbo culture, but is frowned at in the western world as child abuse. The school teacher was not questioned for padding a pupil or student. Some padding was even dished out as parents witnessed, and there was no litigation or appearance before school board. The role of a good adult is paramount in shaping the child into responsible individuals, and that is the responsibility of everyone in the village, not just the parents alone.

EZI NA ULO

Ezi na ulo concept was academically well treated by Dr. Uchendu in the Ahiajoku lectures series of 1995, but in a very difficult style. If we are interested in furthering our understanding of the Igbo culture through analysis and explanation as is the case here, we have to come down from the pulpits of huge lecture halls, sit in the company of the laity, with our legs criss-crossed, and them in un-intimidating atmosphere, explain and teach and create interest. Ezi na ulo is not different from ezi-n'ulo, which is the family. Ezi (compound) and Ulo (house) may not be translated literarily, otherwise the phrase loses its meaning in Igbo context.

In his effort to explore the different layers of meanings that are embedded in the concept of ezi na ulo, and how these help to shape the Igbo cultural life and civilization, Dr. Uchendu introduced two arguments; One, In the study of man, in which Clifford Geertz (1975: 33) argues that the explanation of cultural behavior often consists of "substituting complex pictures for simple ones, while striving somehow to retain the persuasive clarity that went with simple ones." That social scientists tend to "seek complexity and order it." The second position, was a contrarian argument by Whitehead that natural scientists in the process of understanding culture should "seek simplicity and to distrust it" On the other hand, that social scientists tend to "seek complexity and order" (Geertz, 1975: 34). Ezi na ulo interpretation by a non-Igbo makes sense in anthropology, and genealogical discus but is heavily laden with European flavor or under tone.

That Ezi na Ulo, are two clusters of culture traits, embodying material and non-material aspects of the individual, I whole-heartedly agree with. Ezi na Ulo constitute unity and single culture complex in their relevance to Igbo culture. (Uchendu, 1995) Ibo protects and is proud of his ezi na ulo, which includes his family, his property, reputation and status, his territory and boundary.

EXTENDED FAMILY SYSTEM

Every society has an account of the descent of its individual, or family which forms the capacity for constructing and maintaining an extended family. In Igbo land and culture, the extended family phenomenon takes on a different life on its own. A lone successful Ibo man will have his responsibility stretched to generations of big uncles, small uncles, big and small cousins, nephews, distant aunts and nieces. Wherever and whenever there is marriage, there is this element of extended family system because without marriage, there will be no genealogy. Marriage creates four kinship matrices through husband-father, wife-woman, brother-brother, and sister-sister – which are repackaged into eight basic kinship syndromes: husband-wife, father-son, mother-son, mother-daughter, father-daughter, sister-sister, brother-brother, and brother-sister. The Igbo society claims more of these basic structures but decides how much importance to attach to each of them. The father-son and brother-sister emphases provide directions in the two contrasting Igbo kinship structures, therefore giving more focus and direction to this basic important structure. Your wife will always introduce you to a new cousin, a nephew, the grand son or super niece of the grand mother from her maternal lineage, and you must accept them all.

Extended family has been described as a kinship unit with four major characteristics: a unit marked by geographic propinquity (nearness of blood) of occupational integration, strict authority of the presiding elder or patriarch over the component nuclear families and stress on the extended rather than the nuclear family relations. It is a social system lacking a fixed number of specifiable positions (example, husband, father, wife, mother, etc.) but consisting of two or more familiar positions of which one or more resulting dyad is not a nuclear dyad. (husband and wife or two individuals maintaining a sociologically significant relationship). As a social system , it is marked by persistent patterns of social relationship which prevail from generation to generation. As an on-going social unit, extended family commands certain resources (facilities and a territorial base) and certain integrative mechanisms and sanctions such as norms, power, status and prestige which facilitate the attainment of its objectives. (Uchendu, 1971: 183-185).

IGBO WOMEN

In kinship domain, distinction is made between two categories of women in Igbo society:

UMU OKPU – lineage women who may be married, unmarried, divorced or widowed

NDOM / NDINYOM / NDI ALU ALU – belong to the lineage by marriage

First wife (Nwanyi lolo) in Igbo community ranks highest no matter her age or other social disabilities. In the public domain, the sex linked roles, which clearly foster sex segregation, have a leveling effect of leaving women and men to manage their own affairs. Igbo women have the freedom and opportunity to engage in trade on their own account. Wealthy Igbo women, in their roles as "social fathers", traditionally contracted legal marriage with other women and enjoyed all the rights and privileges of husband, except the role of genitor. Women marriage (Uchendu, 1968) enabled wealthy women to convert their wealth into one of the most prestigious rights of Igbo society – the exercise of rights in the reproductive powers of women. It is important here to stress that marriage is associated with sex, but should not be confused with husband and wife's mutual access to sex.

FESTIVALS

The rituals and ceremonies of seasonal festivals in Igbo society are attempts to ensure the continuation of eternal cycle of the seasons, so that crops, animals and man might once again be renewed and revived. If man would sit back and think, the Earth provides everything we need. When the primitive man was hungry, there was animal that could be hunted or edible plant that could be gathered for food. When he was thirsty, there were and still are streams and rivers whose water he could drink. In fact, man was attuned to natural rhythms for instance, the coming of darkness and the light, so he knew when to sleep and when to wake.

A time of celebration in Igbo land is always marked by special observances. As in other cultures, Ibos always celebrate something; birth of a baby, naming ceremony, marriage, graduation, holidays, and especially, the New Yam festival. New Yam festival is not a party, it is an anticipated festivity hugely observed differently form the way to which the visitor is accustomed.

New Yam Festival is celebrated in most parts of Nigeria, but in Okigwe the celebration marks the beginning of a season of plenty and an end to the period of hunger. It is a festival that marks the completion of serious farm work, where the men usually planted yam and women sowed the cocoyam and other crops. Celebration of the new yam is the official announcement that new yam could be eaten and sold in and around Okigwe. The significance of the celebration in retrospect may be emphasized at differing magnitudes throughout the country. In the spirit of oneness, love and enthusiasm, the Ibo offers the new yam to one and all as a reminder once again, the significance of this festival to the African and the cradles of civilization. New Yam festival, as many African festivals is an elaborate celebration, as well as a ritual of dramatic performance, an integral, dynamic part of our culture. This occasion yearns for and earns spontaneous response annually and the people gratefully appreciate the spontaneity and response.

Historically, early Ibos were yam farmers and oil palm producers, so most festivals in Igbo land are geared toward crop cycles. The high priest (Aka-ji-ofor) will eat up the last yams in his barn (Obaa-ji) and awaits the full moon to appear in order for him to inform the people on first of four such announcements before the event. New Yam festival is observed between the months of July and August, and it lasts for eight (8) days in Okigwe. Most towns hold their celebrations at different times (depending on their customary market days), to accommodate their neighboringvillages and to celebrate with them in giving thanks to the gods and ancestors. The period of new yam festival is filled with activities for both the young and old, and it consists of purification rites (n ghu cha) presentation and divining rituals, masquerades and thanksgiving rites. It is considered a taboo to eat new yam before the festival because yam is a sacred crop in Igbo land. Very early in the morning of the first day of the festival, the high priest will sound the wooden gong to summon the village heads (Ndu-isi-ala or Aka-Ji-Ofor), who are also titled men (Nze na Ozo).

They gather at the shrine headquarters, and the high priest sacrifices the biggest goat in the land, sprinkling the blood over a symbol of the god of harvest. Also a cock (big rooster chicken) will be sacrificed, with the blood and feathers sprinkled over the ancestral pots surrounding the shrine.

The goat meat is cooked while yam is boiled and pounded into foofoo form.

After the high priest prays for a better harvest in the coming year he declares the feast open by eating of the pounded yam and goat meat/chicken soup. Every member of the titled men join in, and there comes dancing, palm wine drinking and merrymaking. Most people eat the cooked sliced up yams that are not pounded into foofoo.

To start the week-long festival, a 50 foot ring is build around the shrine with yellow palm fronds from palm trees, with the god of harvest and family members on display for public viewing. Villagers and people from neighboring towns bring presents to the gods and ask for better andbigger harvests, fertility and protection in the coming year. The ritual is that each family or household presents 8 new yams to the family god, cutting off small slice from the heads and tails.

The yams are then cooked with palm oil and chicken, and the symbolic meal is served. The chicken drumsticks are reserved for children as they visit their maternal families to ask for these drumsticks, as their right. After the festival, new yam officially may be eaten by anyone in the community and sold in the village markets. The New Yam Festival is a time of generosity and hospitality among fellow villagers, relatives, friends and in-laws; a cultural event and happiest of ceremonies in Okigwe.

These rituals and cult procedures vary according to the extent of sacrifice and spiritual solicitation. The offer of kola nuts, fresh palm wine, blood of slaughtered rooster and pieces of the new yam by the chief priest or the oldest member of the family is consistent.

The feast of the new yam is a time when the Ibos give thanks to soil (Ala) the earth goddess that nurtures the yam planted on the land, and (Igwe)the sky god that sent the rain that watered the yam. The earth goddess is believed to be the source of fertility and the ultimate judge of morality and conduct (Achebe, 1959)

NEW YAM FESTIVAL
Photo: bbc.co.uk

PALM WINE (MMANYI NKWU)

Palm wine is customary, locally produced and constitutes the principal beverage for adults at dinner and super. It is got from the top part of the palm tree, by tapping it, and fastening a medium sized gourd to it. Some trees can yield two gallons of wine or more within a twelve hour period. A fresh palm wine is deliciously sweet and could be enjoyed by anyone, young or old.

After a few days, palm wine acquires acidic and more spirituous flavor, and such dry taste is enjoyed by the mature old men of the village. At this stage of fermentation, the taste is considered too strong for the women and children who prefer the sugary taste of freshly tapped palm wine.

The talent of palm wine tapping is rare, and not for those afraid of heights. This could turn out to be a trade for the palm wine taper, as advanced orders are placed with them by quite a few competing purchasers, especially during festivities and special occasions. Palm wine is alcoholic that is why it is never served to children. They may be allowed to just taste it but can only drink water and juice. Women are restricted from drinking alcohol, but if they do, it must be in moderation and has to be on a unique and special occasion.

Onye na a dowa mmanyi ura, o nwekwere umu nna?

A man who has fermented wine does not have neighbors

The Igbo saying is in a question form – but literarily means that Ibos call on family members and neighbors to come and drink palm wine if he has more than enough for himself.

A woman does not sit around with men to drink palm wine. She is extended an invitation to where men are drinking. If she politely accepts, she must get down on one knee drink the wine, a glass or two, hand over the glass, get up on her feet, thank the male folks and leave the room. She has not come to engage in conversation, nor is she to sit around and listen to what is being discussed. It is the same expectation in any important family or social event.

NIGERIAN PALM WINE HARVESTER
(Acrylic on canvas)

COLLECTING PALM WINE ON PALM TREE
PALM WINE TAPPER (Picture by: Marco Schmidt, cc. by sa2.5)

This palm wine tapper is holding his wine-tapping knife with his teeth, so that he will have full grasp of the climbing rope (ete) as he climbs up the tree. He might need the knife to open up the tree hole from which the palm wine trickles into his holding container. Notice also that around his waste he is carrying an empty container for bringing down harvested palm wine from the tree.

ENTERPRENEURESHIP

It is a unique and special trade to make climbing rope. The man goes into the forest and chooses the particular climbing stems that are malleable and could easily be pounded and beaten into spongy ropes. They scrape and twist and configure these twisted spongy stems into decent looking climbing instruments, and put them on display for sale. This is a very important one-man industry, and has been for centuries. It is a craft that will never be out-sourced or threatened by technology. It is also a seller's market, made of local raw materials size is individually adjustable.

Climbing rope is made of four vine ropes twisted around each other to a length, for individuality. It is coupled and uncoupled to hug the palm tree while clasping the lower back of the climber. The Igbo man climbs the palm tree to harvest ripe oil palm nuts, with sharp long-broad machete. There is fierce competition at harvesting of oil palm nuts, so the skilled climber is hired from the neighboring village or town, and he is paid by the number of heads of oil palm nuts he could cut down for the hirer. Harvesting palm wine takes an easier approach, because the harvester is self-employed and taps the wine three times a day, while harvesting oil palm nuts is done monthly.

FARMING TOOLS AND EQUIPMENTS

BELLOW –
AN INTEGRAL TOOL FOR A BLACKSMITH

In the background a blacksmith at work, fitting a horse-shoe on farm animal.

Bellows were used to keep the blacksmith's fire burning and very hot by pumping air into it. The Blacksmith made shoes for farm horses, mended farm equipment and made metal farmgates either on his workshop or on the farm. In Igbo land particularly, blacksmith made hoes, machete, spears, arrows, kitchen knives, iron-pots, shovels, buckets, cups, shotguns, hand pistols, bullets, metal drums for palm oil processing and transportation. They also welded kitchen utensils and made traps for animals.

A BLACKSMITH HARD AT WORK
AND HIS APPRENTICES
(Picture from: Matrix.msu.edu) Center for African Studies

Highly skilled metal smiths developed stronger and more efficient Agricultural tools and produced improved weapons.

A Blacksmith displays a few farm
equipments for sale at his workshop

Picture: (Matrix.msu.edu) Center for African Studies.

CHAPTER TWENTY-THREE

GESTURES

Gestures are important communications symbols that people very much rely on. Just imagine yourself watching a Major League Baseball game on television in the United States of America, the catcher is squatting a few feet behind the batter, and you can not help but watch how many fingers and what such mean to the pitcher on the mound. The baseball instance is for illustration purpose, because signs are different from gestures, and must not be confused to mean the same Gestures are also used among the Ibos to express or emphasize an idea. Besides, you are considered wild and undisciplined if you shout out people's names in public.

Different countries have different gestures, or the same gestures may have different meanings in different countries. Voids in knowledge of language cannot be filled with gestures and hand signals, for these can be socially suicidal. Gestures that serve one purpose at a time may be unacceptable in a totally different situation. Do not imitate a gesture unless you understand it, and you are operating within close friends and associates. To be on the safe side make sure you know who can use a certain gesture, and its appropriateness in terms of time. You must use gestures only at the appropriate social levels, if there is no doubt in your mind, whatsoever, that you learned it correctly.

SAFE, COMMON GESTURES

To signal one to for example "come here" which is translated as "bia n'ebe a," hold forearm up, palm facing away from you and slightly inclined, move the fingers down into the palm, then up, repeating the motion.

To gesture "you, come here" as picking a particular young lady or someone from a group, translated: "Gi, bia n'ebe a," hold forearm up, point your index finger in the desired direction, then with the palm away from you and slightly inclined, move the four fingers down in the palm, then up, repeating the motion until the person acknowledges the gesture.

To say by way of gesture "good bye" translated "ka emesia," hold up your forearm, palm away from you, wave the open palm from side to side just from the wrist, or even from the elbow, repeating the motion.

To gesture money or indicate "money" translated "Ego," with the palm facing upward and both index and middle fingers primed together, rub the thumb over the tip of the middle or both fingers three times.

To indicate disdain or dislike of a person or behavior translated "O masighi m," hold the palm facing downward, slightly hold the top of your nose with the thumb and index fingers. This could be an extreme case of dislike, otherwise you could turn your face away your and wave palm two times in dismissal.

To gesture that someone is short "Onyne nke nke or onye mkpu mkpu," hold the palm facing downward, a little above your rib-cage for a few seconds.

To indicate "height of a tall person" translated "onye ogologo," hold palms facing downward, raising your hand above your head

To indicate "sleep or readiness to go to bed" "oge ura" or "oge ula," put palms together, with the fingers opposing each other, bend the wrist of the left hand, move both hands to the left and rest your hand on the back of your right palm.

To gesture small amount "obere ihe," hold the hand up in front of you facing palm sideways, curl the last three fingers into the palm, with the thumb and index finger parallel to each other, with less than an inch of space between them. Another way to gesture the same would be to hold your hand up in front of you, palm facing sideways. Curl the last three fingers into the palm, extend the index finger and with the thumb and index finger of the left palm hold barely the tip of the index finger.

To disagree or gesture "No" translated "mba" "mba" "mba," shake your head vigorously from left to right

To indicate "Yes" by means of gesture, blink your eyes consciously once and nod your head in an up and down motion

To advice someone to "be careful" in the of gesture translated "Ji ri nwa ayo" or "We re nwa ayo," (this gesture could also mean "Take your time" or "Do not be in such a hurry" or "Do not panic") again, hold your palms in front of you, with the fingers and thumb opposing each other, slightly touching your lips with your thumbs, as if in a praying stance.

Note: If any of these gestures seem close or identical to gestures in other culture or language, it should be considered coincidental.

EYE CONTACTS

Ibos like to make eye contacts. A good eye contact is always a welcome sight, and is generally complemented by genuine smile of acknowledgement. Un-complemented eye contact will make a proud Ibo uncomfortable, because it will be interpreted as staring. Sometimes smiling may be misconstrued as insecurity, so it is necessary to smile when appropriate. Eye contacts lasting more than five seconds is considered wrong because it passes the comfort zone, and then again is considered as staring. When you meet an Igbo girl, especially the beautiful and available one, and you make eye contact, it is important to pay attention to her eye brows and work with what she offers you emotionally, a smile, a surprise or sadness. If she opens her mouth to talk, it pays for you to listen, accompanied with a nod of the head at the points of infection. As a foreigner or stranger you will not be dismissed or abandoned too easily. Eye contact is considered the most powerful of all the ways we communicate to other people.

In the Hispanic world, maintaining eye contact in conversation is considered a sign of sincerity, but in some situations, such as facing superiors, parents and teachers, lowering the eyes shows respect, not lack of it or guilt- (Noble, Judith: 1991).

In Igbo society, maintaining eye contact is considered confrontational because Ibos read meanings by so doing and very easily discern facial expression. A parent feels threatened and disrespected if his child maintains eye contact when scolded for an infraction, and slighted if the same child looks away. The child must lower his head and listen quietly, and remain motionless.

CHAPTER TWENTY-FOUR

GOVERNMENT

Nigeria has federal, state and local governments. It has a Republican type of government. On October 1, 1960, the Federation of Nigeria achieved independence from Britain. Nigeria's ethnic, regional, and religious tensions were magnified by the disparities in economic and educational development. The Constitution of the Federal Republic of Nigeria was adopted on October 1, 1963. The government of the Federal Republic of Nigeria extends to all the states, including all member states of Igbo land. In other words, the states are answerable to the federal. First there were three regions, East, West and Northern. Later the three regions were carved into twelve states, and today, the twelve states carved out of three regions have further been carved into thirty-six states. The population has mushroomed to 120 million based on recent 2006 census.

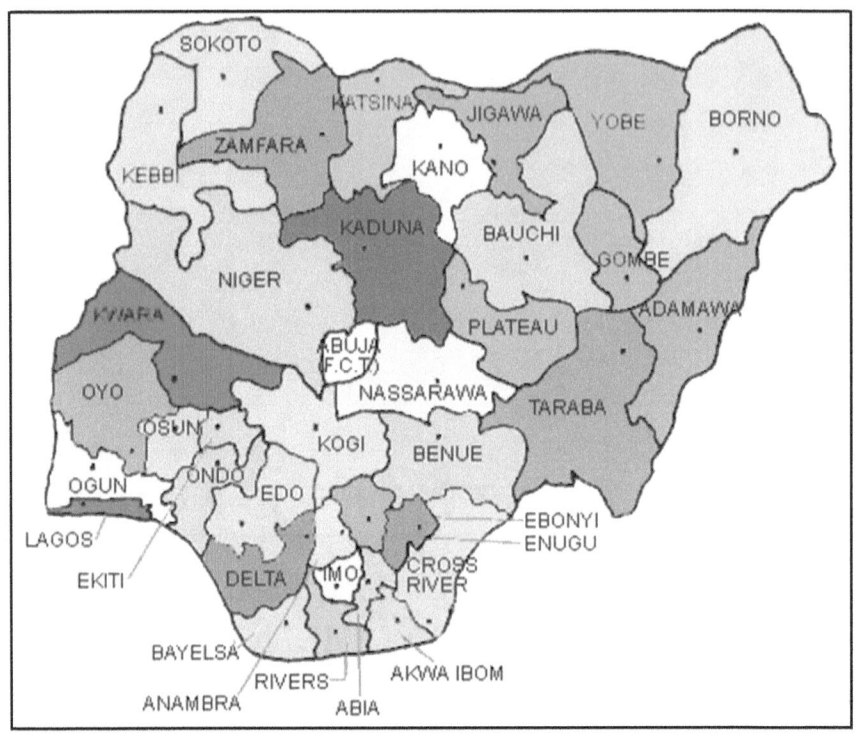

THE 36 STATES OF THE FEDERAL REPUBLIC OF NIGERIA

EVENTS LEADING TO CIVIL WAR -.1966

Nigeria has for some time been characterized as the most populous country in Africa, and dubbed considerably as the continent's most powerful nation. It became independent on October 1, 1960.

As a federation it had distinctively three regions, the Eastern Region; the Western Region; and the Northern Region. The Northern Region was dominated by the Hausa people, the Western Region by the Yoruba people, while the Eastern Region was dominated by the Ibo people.

The Ibos believe in community, so would rally together to put a single bright child through school; and when the graduate had secured a position of power, he would help find jobs his kinsmen who sacrificed to make his success possible. It so happened that after the British handed over power to Nigeria the Ibos inherited the control of the civil service system, dominating key posts in government, the army, police and major corporations. This controlling influence of the Ibos did not endear them to the rest of the country, especially the Northerners.

The Lugard amalgamation policy of 1914, deliberately kept the North separate from the South, isolating the North from the impact of Southern economic activity, Christian influence and educational progress. Christian missionary schools educated people in the South areas and made them progressively minded. On the other hand, Muslim areas especially in the North almost entirely confined to Islamic schools that did not prepare for modern professions.

In efforts to reconcile the ambitions of rival regional and tribal groups a coalition government was set up, to represent the Northern Region, the Eastern Region and the Western Region. Dr. Nnamdi Azikiwe represented the Ibos of the East, Sir Abubakar Tafawa Balewa represented the Northerners who were the majority, while Chief Obafemi Awolowo from Western Region represented the Yoruba people. Under this arrangement, Dr. Nnamdi Azikiwe became President, Sir Tafawa Balewa became Prime Minister, and Chief Awolowo, led the Opposition party.

On a January day in 1966, the army successfully wrestled power of governance from civilians in a military coup. Following the January 1966 military coup, northern tribal animosity against the Ibo-dominated government led to anti-Ibo riots in the North. In Kano a major city in the North Ibos were massacred in the hundreds without warning, information or provocation. Thousands were repossessed of their homes and property. Major General Aguiyi Ironsi, the highest ranking Ibo man in the Army was in control at this time, as Head of State of the Federal Republic of Nigeria. Major General Ironsi was assassinated later that year when the Northerners staged an carried out successfully a counter coup and Col. Yakubu Gowon became the Head of State.

Northerners tried to justify the July 29, 1966 coup when they said that General Aguiyi Ironsi was too moderate on them, considering their atrocities on the Ibos that they feared some other radical Ibo man in the military might overthrow him.

As soon as the Northerners regained complete control of government under Gowon's leadership a new upheaval began. Northern civilians and army units slaughtered over thirty thousand Ibos in different cities in the North. and berserk Muslim mobs and mutinous Hausa soldiers continued the mutilation of hundreds of thousands more. They had all the guns and ammunition and they saw an opportunity to be reckless with weapons on civilians all over the Northern Region of Nigeria.

Northern Muslim mobs and Hausa soldiers hacked Ibos to pieces in offices, in their homes, at their businesses, at airports and at railroad stations as they attempted to escape with nothing but their lives. This began the exodus of the Ibos to their homelands in Eastern Region of Nigeria.

Civil war broke out as Gowon attacked the Eastern "rebellion" hoping for a brief "surgical police action." Lt Col. Ojukwu counter attacked, invading federal troupes, and this led to one of the bloodiest civil wars in modern history. The tool in human lives and economics was greag on the Ibo nation.

IMAGES OF BIAFRA/NIGERIA CIVIL WAR – 1966 - 1970

CHAPTER TWENTY-FIVE

OFFICIAL LEGAL TENDER (NIGERIAN CURRENCIES) THE NAIRA AND KOBO

Naira and kobo are the official legal tender in Nigeria, but given the valuation of the money, as a result of devaluation by the International and World Bank, the purchasing power is negligent that the kobo are rarely used, or even seen. The denominations are in N5, N10, N20, N50, N100, N500, and N1000. They circulate the pictured heads of dead presidents, heads of State and some other significant Nigerians.

Naira is divided into 100 kobo.

Coins are in denominations of N1, 50, 25, 10, 1.

**Herbert Macaulay - a strange fellow on the
One Naira currency.**

It is a wrong choice in my opinion, because he was no George Washington for Nigeria. His name is European too, it is no wonder the one Naira currency is installmentally going extinct because of its purchasing power.

NIGERIA 10 NAIRA 2000
Front: Dr. ALlvan Ikoku (1900-1971) Back: Fulani Milk Maids

Chief Obafemi Awolowo

Nigeria 200 Naira 2000
Front: Alhaji Sir Ahmadu Bello (1909- 1966)
Back: Agricultural Commodity and Livestock Farming

DR. NNAMDI AZIKIWE

This is a very strange arrangement on the front of a national currency. Two heads are definitely not better than one in this situation. Political correctness is taken to the extreme in an effort to please or to put a front. I would advise otherwise, and that is what is called MAKING A DECISION

NIGERIA 1000 NAIRA 2005
FRONT: ALHAJI ALIYU MAI-BORNU AND DR. CLEMENT ISONG (Former Governors of the Central Bank of Nigeria)

The one thousand Naira was released into circulation on October 2005. This is the highest denomination of Nigerian currency in circulation.

CHAPTER TWENTY-SIX

PUNCTUALITY

Igbo people have, in differing degrees, a perception of time that is different from Europe or the United States of America. Punctuality is enforced at meetings by the imposition of fines, otherwise an Igbo man may show up at meetings two hours late, and refuses to understand the consequences. Ibos who have been invited for 5: 00 p.m. party on a Saturday evening event may not begin to arrive until 6: 30 p.m. or later. In fact, there is a term for it, it is called "African time". A few of us are actually embarrassed when non-Africans who are invited to somewhere arrive, and stand around to complain about other engagements they would have attended prior, if they knew how later our parties start as against the time on their invitations.

However, storekeepers and places of business open always on time. Schools are strict on punctuality and stick to schedules, but to public transport systems, and church services, especially when the congregation has to wait for the priest to arrive, punctuality is unheard of.

ROLE OF RELIGION

Numerously, religion has popped up in discussion of Igbo Culture and tradition in this book because religion has traditionally played a very vital role in the social life and the every day activities of the Igbo people of Southeastern Nigeria. Detailed discussion follow later.

In fact, not overtly religious activities may begin with prayers, or other religious manifestations, such as blessing, as in the presentation of the "kola nut"; at dinner tables and at parties, or before the Ibo goes to bed at night. A mass may be said when an Ibo man is leaving to overseas institution of higher learning, at burial ceremony or even a new home may be blessed.

In the domain of religion, Igbo people have a great passion to "find out" the wishes of the gods or ancestors who have sent us a symbolic message. Consulting a diviner may be one alternative source of communicating with them; going into trance, or to one of the major oracles in Igbo land may be others – (Uchendu; 1965: 187-97.

GREETINGS

There are several ways the Ibos salute people at meetings. Most people express good wishes in the English way, although the sound is quite different to the foreigner.

Unu abuola chi	good morning
Unu aputala ura	good morning
Ehihe oma	good afternoon
Kedu ka unu di	how are you - plural
Mma mma nu	You are looking good - plural
Unu anuo la	How are you – plural
Ana m ekele unu	I salute you
Ekele diri unu	greetings to you – plural
Ndi be anyi unu anuo la	How are you, my people
Ka chi buo	Good night

Ka chi fuo "
Buo nu chi "
Ka oduwa ubochi ozo   Till next time

    The above are phrases that serve as salutations at meetings. People use them to greet each other while passing or as they shake hands before starting a conversation. If you want to acknowledge others without stopping, you may say:

      Ka emesia
      A ga na ahu
      A ga ahukorita

      We shall see
      We shall meet again

    If someone meets you while you are eating or about to eat, at social event, crowded gathering, festivals, and much more elaborate circles, such bodies are greeted thus:

      Igbo Kwenu
      Igbo Kwenu!
      Okigwe Knenu!
      Kwezuenu!

Each of the greetings is responded with a resounding Yaa!

PUBLIC ADDRESS SYSTEM

In most gatherings, if you want to be heard or permission to say something or to address the audience and people do not seem to give you the time of the day, there are several ways you can greet them:

> 1. "Igbo kwenu! Kwe kwa nu!! Kwe zuo nu!!!

They will respond at each chant, and at the end of the third, everyone's eyes and ears are focused on you or your direction. This is the Western equivalent of (Hip, hip, hurray!)

> 2. "Che- che-che-nu, mma mma nu! (the response is a
>   resounding Yaa!)
> "Mma mma nu!! (the crowd once again responds with a
>   louder Yaa!
> "Kwezuo nu!!! (the gathering response again is Yaa!!)

This is the unwritten three chant law of the Igbo society. The speaker has gotten the attention he demanded by the first chant, and by the second, more people become aware and he asks for permission to speak, and by the third chant, he is confirming that everyone has agreed to hear him speak.. The speaker then grees the gathering, introduces himself and commences to say what he wants to tell the public.

> In some parts of the Igbo land:
> "Onye na nke ya, onye na nke ya"
> is a way of greeting people en masse
> (All for one, one for all)

> In other parts of the land:
> "Ndi be anyi unu anwuna"
> May you not die, my brethren!
> Umu nna m, unu anwuchula onwu!
> My people, may you not die premature death!
> Umu nna m, birikwa nu o!
> My people, you must live long life!

TELEPHONE SERVICE

Telephone Service in Igbo land and Nigeria for that matter is different from what obtains in the United States. The State controls the telephone service although recently private international conglomerates are making inroads. People answer the telephone just the same as in any English speaking society. They will answer hello…..! and when a voice is unfamiliar would say…who is calling…..! Onye na akpo…!

There are three types of telephone service in Igbo land and Nigeria for that matter. The first is called "land phone" which is the telephone service wired to individual homes. Experience is that land phone calls are cheaper per minute than the other services I am about to mention. The other is "Business center" phone calls….! Here, anyone who wants to make telephone calls simply go to a vendor, call out the telephone numbers to be dialed and when connection is made, the vendor hand the telephone receiver to the customer and starts immediately to time the call to be charged per minute. How much do I owe you, will be the question to ask the vendor? Ego ole ka m ji gi.?

The vendor calculates to the nearest minute, and gets paid. Some of these vendors are on the roadside, while there are well established businesses who also offer internet phone services.

The third type of telephone service in Igbo land is the "hand set". Almost everyone now has it nowadays, whether or not it is operational. There are no monthly service charges for use, no packaged deals like one would expect from AT&T, or Pacific Bell or Sprint/Nextel, rather the hand sets are designed to use sim-cards, which is a prepayment arrangement lasting as long as the amount you paid for the card. When your credit is used up, you may receive calls but cannot place a call to no one. In the villages, people may not have chargers for their hand-sets, and may have trouble locating a place to charge their hand-sets. When this is the situation, the caller might not panic because it is a known problem.

TELEPHONE DIRECTORY

There are no telephone directories that would list individual addresses and phone numbers, except for businesses and government entities. People call only those numbers they have of friends, relatives or businesses. Telephone companies do sometimes assign on telephone number to as many as five different households, but this problem is disappearing since the country has been flooded with hand-sets (cell-phones) from Europe.

CHAPTER TWENTY-SEVEN

HOUSING

Homes usually have courtyards. In the rural communities, single family houses are built facing the streets. Walls are built to enclose the backyard, kitchen and den for animals. Kitchens are built away from the main house. During the olden days, the family head usually the husband man has a large square piece of ground, surrounded with a walled fence or enclosed with a wall made of earth tempered, which hardens as brick when dry. Today's buildings on the other hand are so sophisticated that the new generation of Ibos will have a hard time understanding any description of a typical house built in the early 1800s in a typical Igbo village. Houses do not share walls with neighbors' buildings. Usually there are vegetable gardens behind the family houses, and flowers in front that give the homes quite an inviting look. Shade trees are also planted around the houses, but mostly shade trees of choice are the fruit bearing trees that serve also as cash crops.

Examples include citrus trees, mango pears, palm trees, coconuts, banana and cola trees. Houses have two-sided and four-sided roofs.

There are open space areas in front of the buildings called mbara ezi. Many buildings have grillwork over the windows on the upper floors, as well as balconies, and veranda around the houses on the ground floors. In the cities, buildings with stalls and stores on the ground floors often have living quarters on the upper floors. High rise residences may have penthouses that have openings to the roof up to the sky and serve as patios in some cases, and a way to provide light and air. Interior of buildings floors are plastered with cement or glazed ceramic floor tiles or tarrazzoo mables. The walls of many kitchens are made of red bricks or covered with glazed ceramic wall tiles. The designs and patterns come in different geometric shapes and in varying colors. People use pieces of furniture to store clothing, jewelry boxes, trunk boxes portmanteaux and luggage. Storage niches are made in the walls and some closets made by walling off a corner of the room, or at the foot of canopy bed railings.

KITCHEN

In most villages the kitchen is built behind the main family house, as food is prepared away from view of most visitors. Things have changed and most modern single or multi family buildings are as any you can find in California or any other part of the United States. A visitor to a home may not go to the kitchen, unless invited or with permission. Women used t exercise authority over everything in the kitchen. It was considered the domain of the woman of the house. Again this changed when men took their wives to live with them in America. The tasks that were looked upon as women's work are now done mostly by men. Men cook dinner nowadays for the family and especially for their wives in America especially if the feminine kind happens to work outside of the home, or brings any semblance of pay-check, monthly. The situation is worse if there are children involved. The children even look up to their fathers to cook them something, and sometimes complain to their mother that their father did not cook them something. Cook them something means cook something for them to eat. It must be emphasized that typical situation described occurs even when the Americanized Ibo wife is home all day, probably sleeping in the next room. There are however, exceptional ladies who do it all tirelessly without regrets.

CHAPTER TWENTY-EIGHT

PEOPLE'S NAMES

It is the tradition that the full name of an Ibo man consist of the first, which is the baptismal name, followed by the vernacular name, usually the name the parents give to their young at birth, which we write nowadays as middle name and lastly the surname, usually the father's family name. Personally I would advocate that the intellectual community start a movement to rid the Igbo of English names. This process may have started but been slow and very individualistic and besides, changing names has never been our way of life. Most Igbo names start with vowels – A, E, I, O, U and I have not been able to find the underlying significance or why it is so. Igbo names have distinctive meanings that tell a lot about a family, the child or circumstances surrounding birth. Some Igbo names are historical or derivative of the days of the week. If a woman marries, she would automatically drop her surname on the day of marriage and take the surname of the husband.

OKORO is the most popular surname in the land to the extent that other ethnic Nigerians would call an Ibo man "okoro mmadu" to imply Ibo man. There are several explanations to the Okoro name, one being that the original ancestor believed in family that during his first contact with another human identified himself as a "Okoro" meaning group, in his effort not to exclude his family, hence he became known as OKORO. There has never been any record of this anywhere till now for the fact that we have but oral history of the Igbo people and culture.

My source was Nze Ogbuagu Aguguo of Okai Village in Umuna Okigwe of Imo State, Nigeria who died at the age of 115 years in the year 2000. This I was told during my visit to his house December, 1995 in a conversation with him about unrelated topic altogether.

Another name that one identifies with the Ibo man is "IKE" which means Energy. It could also mean power. In Igbo golden saying "Ike is the essence of all things human, spiritual, animate and inanimate. Literally, this means that everything has its own unique energy. Another golden saying, I also call proverb of interest in regard, is that "power runs in many channels." Literally translated as meaning that a mild and gentle child could be a giant killer. Power, therefore may mean authority, jurisdiction, control but should not always be seen in terms of physical strength or awe-some-ness.

FIRST NAMES

A person's first name is usually the name given to him at baptism. Most baptismal names are taken from the bible as people research to find the most appealing or fitting names for their baby. Some first names are suggested by the clergy, an authority in the church or by a literate person in the family. These names are mostly names of biblical saints like John, Christopher, Gabriel, Peter, Joseph, Theresa, Paul, Mary Matthew, Francis and Michael. Some names simply have religious significance or derived from Latin language for instance Columbus, a Latin gender meaning "of the dove." Dove is the bird of peace and very few people ask or know why doves are released to fly away at very significant peace processes or the like events and sometimes delivering olive branch. The name Columbus was derived from Latin word Columba meaning dove or Columbus, of the dove. Lately, people name their first born sons after themselves especially on the father's side, junior this junior that and junior everything, as a means to seek the immortality of their names. Unfortunately, this is not so with the feminine kind. Firstborn daughters are not given their mother's first names. The women' liberation are yet to touch that. When a child has the same first name as the father, it is customary for the child to be called by a diminutive form of the name for example:

Obele
Nwanna
Nwoke-nta
Oyiri nna ya
Junior or Jr.
Mba-ike

First names were not exactly first names per say. When an Ibo child is born, he or she is given a name like Onwujekwe, Chukwuemeka, Iheanyichukwu, Onyemauchechukwu, Ngeremchi, Adamma, Iheanacho, etc. So, the middle names we use today as our middle names, and in majority of times initialed was the first names we were given by our parents, then in later days or weeks, months or years when the child is baptized, he or she takes on a Christian name at baptism. Because baptism was a milestone for the Ibo youth or for the young parents, it was common practice to inform everyone that the child's original sin has been washed away, along with Ibo name which was termed "heathen". The proud parents tender the baptismal certificates as they petition for change of names. That was how first names given to Ibo children are now middle names, and in most situations are only used as middle initials.

People who chose to have two surnames usually write their father's names followed by their father's last names. In all communities of Igbo land people may have double last names. Both names of the families of husband and wife are not represented. Women change their last names after marriage, and their children do not get new blended last names. Igbo people are called by their husbands' last names which happen to be the name the children will be called.

POPULAR IGBO NAMES AND THEIR MEANINGS

MALES

Amaechi	Who knows tomorrow
Onyemaechi	Who knows tomorrow
Amaechi	Family name will not be lost
Amaefule	I will never lose my place
Anyaegbu	Looks alone can't kill
Azubike	Your backing is your strength
Chidimma	God is good
Chijioke	Wealth is God's to give
Chinedu	God leads
Chinweokike	God alone creates (creation is God's)
Chika	God is greatest or God is supreme
Chioma	Good God
Chukwudi	There is God
Chukwuemeka	God has done wonderful things for us
Chukwuma	God knows
Chukwunyere	God's gift
Chinyere	God's gift
Eberechukwu	God's grace
Iheanyichukwu	Nothing is impossible with God
Ikemefule	May my strength not be lost
Ikenna	God, the almighty father's strength
Kelechi	Give thanks to God
Madueke	Not of man's creation
Maduka	Human life is worth more than wealth
Nnamdi	My father lives/always backs me
Onuoha	Majority has spoken
Obinna	The heart of the father

Obioha	Majority intention of the people
Uchechukwu	God's will
Ugochukwu	God annointed
Nwafor	Born on Afor market day
Nwankwo	Born on Nkwo (a day after Afor market)
Okoronkwo	Born on Nkwo
Okorie/Nwaoye	Born on Orie (day before Afor market)

FEMALES

Adaeze	First daughter of a king (EZE)
Adanze	First daughter of titled man (chieftain)
Adamma	First, yet beautiful daughter
Chiamaka	God is beautiful
Chinyere	God's gift
Chioma	Good God
Chinwendu	God owns all life
Ekwutosi	Don't criticize
Iheoma	Good thing (has happened to us)
Ndidi	Patience
Ngozi	Blessing
Nkeiru	Future holds prosperity
Nwakaego	The child is more than any amount of money
Nwamaka	A child is good to have
Okwuchi	God's pronouncement

CHAPTER TWENTY-NINE

RELIGION AND ART

The Ibos have for a long time been religious people and used all forms of worship to explain the mystery and forces of life and death. There is this very firm belief in the Supreme Being, and the burning desire to please the gods and express their feelings to the gods resulting in great works of art. There is no one traditional religious practice in Igbo land. Before the influence of Europeans and Christian missions, however, most Igbo speaking people practiced some form of ancestor worship, which held that in order to gain success in this life, one must appease of the spirits of the deceased. Interestingly enough, one of the primary ways of accomplishing the appeasement of the deceased is to show respect for the dead through participation in the secret men's society, Mmo.

Different parts of Igbo land use different names to describe this and such similar societies. The second level of these initiates was responsible for carrying out the funeral ceremonies for the deceased and inducting the departed spirits into the ebe mmo, so that they would no longer causemischief in the village. In some areas, the native doctor conducts this induction.

The Ibo worships a creator god called Chukwu or Chineke and countable other spirits and deities who can inhibit or take the form of natural objects and phenomena. There is also a strong belief that the deceased relatives can help protect and guide the Ibo man and that is where the practice of ancestral worship and building shrines to the deceased became common and accepted practice.

Religion and Christianity have been unable to undo this strong belief and practice. Ancestral worship in Igbo land could be credited for the people's strong sense of community, rites of initiation and induction into revered societies. Why initiation….because through initiation an adolescent boy enters into the adult world, and in some cases, into the revered secret societies. Initiations help your men enter into society by instilling in them the values of productivity and social consciousness by strengthening their sense of heritage and community.

The art of Ibo has such representation that it has been characterized as conventional in style. This is so because the pieces of work have always expressed ideas that command very strong foundational belief of the people. The artists attempt to capture as well as celebrate the moral and religious convictions governing the every day life of the individual. The missionaries came, built churches, schools and hospitals, labeled the Africans as primitive and their religion, paganism. As a result, millions of Ibos turned away from their ancestral ways of worship, even changed their names in the process and have become Christians. Christianity has been a great force in the area ever since, and today Christian missionaries are everywhere in Igbo land, fake and real.

The belief in one Creator of all things, who governs events especially life and death, has not changed. In fact history will have it that in 2005, one of our Ibo sons His Highness Archbishop Arinze was so highly placed in the Catholic Church he almost was expected to be chosen as the new Pope and also to be the first black pope ever. An Igbo pope, living at the Vatican City, as the head of the Catholic Church!

Wow!! I am sure he would still get collect calls from distant relatives in Onitsha, who would care little if they woke him up at 3: 20 am. Vatican City time.

Quite a great many Ibos believe in the doctrine of eternity and the transmigration of the departed souls. When a young Ibo dies tragically, relatives claim he has made appearances to them, and the belief was that his spirit is restless because it wasn't time for it to rest peacefully. The non-transmigrated spirits, such as friends and relatives are believed as always attending them and guarding them from bad spirits of their foes. For this reason, before eating they offer a portion of the food to them by putting the food piece on the ground and pouring a few drops of wine on the ground too as a way of inviting them to come and eat. Sometimes the spirits are called upon to come and partake in the meal, without pouring or putting the food or wine away on the ground.

Libations are made after washing hands to eat by pouring drops of wine or any liquid on the floor and tossing a small quantity of the food in a certain place or outside for the spirits of departed relations. The natives suppose the spirits to preside over their conduct and protect them from evil. This may be misconstrued as having or worshipping another god but it is not. During festivals when animals and fowls are slaughtered for the occasions, the blood of these animals are offered as holy gifts on the graves of ancestors and departed spirits. These old forms of worship or oblations are disappearing slowly but the sacred trees are still tended in some rural communities by traditional leaders and shrine heads and chief priests.

In the Catholic Church for instance there are such moments during church services when the priest invokes offering the Eucharistic elements to God and it makes me wonder if there is any difference. The drums are still answered in Igbo land today when they call, and the statues placed in shrines are reverenced and still freshly painted with cam wood yearly, especially before festivities. These great masks are brought out for public display and viewing, and cleaned, polished and dressed up to please the gods. When the Ibo carvers and sculptors make masks or statues, they put all their religious feelings into it as something that is used to please the gods, not for commercial reasons.

CARVED IGBO DOOR

CHAPTER THIRTY

SOCIAL RITUALS OF TRADITIONAL IGBO CULTURE

Rituals are deeply rooted in social customs or may be rites according to religious laws but are always established for ceremony. Social rituals are an important aspect of the Igbo culture, and they can be especially helpful in revealing the core values of many societies. The sharing of the kola nuts constitutes one of the most vital aspects of social and ritual roles in traditional Igbo culture and society. There is an established belief in kola nut divination, which is the customary way of reading how the nuts land after they are tossed. Kola can be given as an offering to the spirits, churches, mosques, or even strangers on the street. The various ideas associated with kola nut allow it to be a part of all traditional in all parts of the Igbo life.

The Ibo makes distinctions based on the color of the kola nut, as the white kola nut symbolizes potential prosperity and social distinction. The four- cotyledon kola nut is more sought after for ritual reasons, because the number four is very sacred to the Ibo. The second in importance of social rituals of traditional Igbo culture is the naming ceremony. "Name-giving" is a formal occasion, celebrated with feasting and drinking, that serves the purpose of expressing the social group to which a child belongs. This takes place eight days (izu ukwu) after a child is born, and the name defines this new life.

NAMING CEREMONY

Igbo names are not given at random, as you will find in other sections of this book. A child is given several names all with very carefully thought out meanings within the familial and social spheres. Concerns for future child, important past historical events in the family or household, preferences for the sex of a child, or other aspects of the current social world at the birth of the child can be relayed through the name. The name may also reflect a chosen ancestor or honor the family legacy.

The offering of kola nuts and yam porridge to family and friends takes place and is used to mark the ceremony. The head of the new born child is shaved, representing a fresh start for the spiritual life of the child. The naming ceremony is a key aspect of Ibo life because of this huge significance in the name. "Our name is our history and our bloodline."

Palm wine, the alcoholic drink of choice for the Ibo, is present at almost all ceremonies and rituals, and is indispensable at such and all social occasions. Ibos use rituals and sacrifices to encourage spiritual benevolence and power that is why at the onset of any palm wine drinking, some of the wine is poured on the ground in homage to the spirits of the departed. I have personally observed where it was deemed necessary to step outside the house to pour wine on the bare ground where the wine will sink through the sand, avoiding the inside that may be cement floor, tiled or covered with carpet. A libation, the act of pouring an alcoholic liquid offering to the spirit, is made as tribute for festive occasions. The time when the sap from palm trees is harvested is a time of great celebration and festivities.

The communication to the Sprits continues through music and dance, with specific rhythms to persuade a particular spirit. In some initiation rites, the initiates will be doused in palm wine from head to foot as part of the process of transition into a specific age group, or society. The significance of the palm wine, just as the kola nuts, help to illustrate a pattern in all Igbo rituals, especially those illustrated above. The Ibo emphasizes the importance of Spirits and the all- important and central role of family and community in everyday lives of its people.

THE KOLA NUT

Kola nut is a native and product of the African tropical agriculture. It has very special significance in the culture of the Igbo land. Kola nut is used as a gesture of peace, and friendship, but most importantly, it is the most prominent symbol of hospitality. Although kola nut has not be proven or otherwise, to have any nutritional value, it is a cash crop, a store of social wealth, and a sign in African Astrology. The belief in kola nut divination, and the various ideas associated with kola nut allow it to be part of almost all traditional parts of the Ibo life.

As a symbol of Igbo hospitality, at any village or town gathering, kola nut is offered to indicate that the matter to be discussed is very important. When a guest visits an Igbo household, there is a compulsive necessity to serve him with kola nuts. The sharing of kola nuts is perhaps one of the most important aspects of social and ritual roles in Ibo society. The offering or presentation of the kola nut is an important ceremony with three main stages that must follow a certain path which helps the Igbo to reinforce their model of social structure, and anyone who fails in any of the vital steps will be penalized by the village elders or titled men present.

The presentation is a privilege of the host and an honor reserved exclusively for men, denied to women on cultural reasons. Kola nut presentation may follow one of the following principles on the commensal group: It may follow the genealogical distance, the social distance, the social differentiation, and the status structure. (Uchendu 1964: 47-50) If the guests are drawn from different Igbo communities, an expanded "model" is invented to accommodate the new situation.

The presentation of kola nut involves passing the kola nuts with the recitation of appropriate proverbs to be followed by a prayer from the oldest member of the host's lineage who is present. The presenter, if at a ceremony holds up the kola and says a prayer to the ancestors. He summons the gods of the ancestors and all the friendly spirits together and asks them to be present at the ceremony. He demands good health for the people and wishes ill health for the enemy, but peace to all in the village and community. Sometimes kola nuts are offered with alligator peppers, (ose orji) and the later is never mentioned as the kola is passed around for all to see and acknowledge, before the kola makes its journey back to the presenter. "Orji nze gaa onye nze n'aka"

The second stage, the breaking of the kola nut, separates the kola into its various cotyledons, follows different patterns depending upon the area of the Igbo land. For the northern Ibo, the breaking should never be delegated to a junior or an inferior, but for the southern Ibo, the separation is labor and thus permissible for a junior to do the breaking as a service to the host.

The distribution of the kola nut, the final stage, follows this pattern, as the host receives the first share of the kola, and each member of this party gets a share in order of seniority.

Kola nuts have cotyledons from the monocotyledon of the "gworo variety to the octo-cotyledon kola, which have eight cotyledons or seed leaves. As mentioned above, the four cotyledon kola nut is more sought after for ritual reasons – the number four being sacred to the Ibo.

(ji ano, ede ano -- orji ano, -- ose ano)

The white kola nut (orji ugo) is a rarity, hence the symbolism invested with it.

Kola nut is very rich in caffeine and it is chewed throughout West Africa. There is a popular African saying that "He who brings kola brings life". It is a stimulant because of its caffeine content. It is believed as one of the main ingredients in the Coca-Cola drinks

"Onye wetara orji wetara ndu"

He who brings kola brings life

Because it is considered sacred, kola nut is used everyday in religious sacrifices, and to bless marriages. It is also believed to cure certain illnesses such as sexual weakness. Unlike Viagra, kola nut does not require doctor's prescription.

KOLA NUTS

ASSORTMENT OF THE KOLA NUTS
AT A MARKET IN IGBOLAND!
Photo by: Bobbie Nystrom of Pidgin Pals

CHAPTER THIRTY-ONE

LEGENDS

A story from the Igbo past, oral history of course, had it that the first European to have ventured into the heartland of the Igbo nation was killed by the natives, because none had seen such a creature before. The name was Bay-kay according to the sense the natives could make of the strange figure's pronouncement when he was asked what his name was. Even today in Igbo land, a white person of European decent is called "Bay-kei ocha or nwa Bay-kay" meaning the son of Baykay. This is as unproven as the UFOs and the Bigfoot legends or Aliens from outer space. Presently, no Igbo community has claimed for its ancestors, the notoriety for the famous supposedly killing.

The first mode of transportation for the first infamous European Mr. Bay-kay was a bicycle. He was considered a premonition; a weird creature they thought could be either a ghost or another form of life that simply strayed, a misfit or ghost on very brief mission.

The villagers hung the bicycle high up in the village square and a huge fire was built directly under it. It was later destroyed because the wheels turning as the bicycle was suspended in the air, frightened the villagers, who feared that the bicycle was running to inform its people that Baykaay had been killed, and that they might come for war in the village. Just as the name Baykaay is what a white person is called in Igbo land, very light-skinned person is also referred to as Baykaay, to indicate that he is like a white person. Also traveling to European countries, including the United States and Canada is also called traveling to "ala Baykaay" white man's land

THE NOK CIVILIZATION

The Nok culture and civilization, according to findings by archeologists was documented as having flourished in Central Nigeria as early as 2000 to 500 B.C. The famous find, "treasure trove of terracotta figurines and portrait heads" were further evidence of artistic skills and achievement of the Ibos that existed hundreds of years before the Greek or Egyptian sculptors and civilization. There are no Igbo legends, no powerful kings, and lack of written records, but Igbo literature is very rich in proverbs, riddles, folk stories and chants, and were passed on from generation to generation over many centuries. African Art has value as entertainment. Some mainly serve political purposes or of ideological significance while others are instruments of ritual context.

Pottery Head found at Nok Nigeria
Viewable today at Jos Museum Height: 21 cm.
Photo by: Frank Willett.

This was reportedly the "earliest known large size sculpture produced in pottery during the 5th Century BC., indicative of the antiquity of many basic canons of West African sculpture".

ORACLE CULT

Ibos relied on a large number of oracles, which they consulted to provide verdicts for numerous disputes that arose in the Igbo society. Anyone consulting the oracle was warned ahead of time that the gods would punish him if he ignores the verdict rendered. The Ibo believed that Chukwu (God) dwelt in a cave somewhere in Aro village, and spoke to the devotees who visited him. A naïve superstition, yet when the oracle had spoken, anyone found guilty was ordered to pay with a number of slaves to be sacrificed to the oracle. These priests (agents) of the oracle never sacrificed anyone to the oracle (deity) rather they actually sold these sacrificial humans to slave merchants.

The oracular cult organizations and their priests often employed mercenaries to burn down villages of those who refused to accept verdicts, and to capture such offenders to be added to the toll of slaves. They used this type of intimidation to ensure that their oracle maintained its reputation. The Aro-Chukwu was considered most objective, because of its remoteness far from the location of disputes, and they also convinced litigants that they have no direct or vested interest in the outcome of disputes.

Aro-Chukwu oracle virtually became the supreme court of the Igbo judicial system, in terms of hearing appeals in important cases from different parts of Igbo land, and levying fines and fees. In later years the Aro-Chukwu oracle exploited its position to become a vital instrument and major player in the slave trade.

THE ARO-CHUKWU ORACLE

Before Christianity took a foothold in Igbo land, pilgrimages were made to a village named Aro where the celebrated shrine of Chukwu was communicated with. People from all parts of Southeastern Nigeria thronged the town because it was believed that God lived there. The Aro oracle dominated the slave trade of the area behind Calabar, but it wasn't the only source of supply. The lack of central authority among the Ibos and the ever constant and unending inter-village disputes, steadily fed the trade. Aro became the most powerful trading community in the entire country in the sixteenth century, because traders from Aro were believed to possess the voice of Chukwu, and for years they held the monopoly of supplying slaves to the Delta states.

Crowds of pilgrim-votaries thronged the shrine and Aro people began systematically exploiting their oracle for profit. Litigants were subjected to systematic economic exploitation. They were not allowed into the town, but forced to wait "the law's delay" in the forest near the cave of Chukwu, where they were sold food and drinks at very high prices for months, until their cases were heard and another gigantic fraud would be perpetrated.

The belief was that after each party has stated its case before the mouth of the cave, Chukwu (God) would speak his verdict from within, and the losing party must then enter the cave to be eaten by Chukwu. The truth was that the oracular priest spoke from within, and when the unfortunate losers entered, they were quickly clubbed and bound by waiting strong arm hench-men, and packed into waiting canoes behind the cave, and shipped down river as slaves.

Records are that in a desperate 1902 attempt and effort to establish control and occupy the Igbo country, "the British forces attacked Aro-Chukwu, and the Chukwu's oracle cave was destroyed and its roof blown off". The British soon realized that to occupy Ibo, unlike other major ethnic groups in the north and west, they had to fight for every village.

The religion of the Igbo was called Pagan by the British. It consisted of numerous rites and ceremonies that in general were of a pre-eminently superstitious character. The Ibo believed in an Almighty being, a common supreme God, omnipresent, and omnipotent, and still do. The people believe that Chukwu or Chineke (God) is responsible for everything in this world and the next.

Relying on a number of oracles, the Chukwu oracle was the dominant high god, worshipped constantly and communicated with through his sacred shrine at Aro. Chukwu-Okike (God the Creator) is still considered the supreme God, and is called different names throughout the Igbo speaking nation.

When a man goes to Aro to consult Chukwu, he is received by the priests outside of the town of Aro, near a small stream. Here he makes an offering, after which a fowl (rooster) is killed, and if it appears unpropitious, (not of good omen) a quantity of red dye is split in the water which the priests tell the people is blood, and on this, the votary is hurried off by the priests and he is seen no more. It was being given out that Chukwu has been displeased and has taken him. The result of this disciplinary ceremony is determined in general by the amount of the present given to the priests, and those who were reported to have been carried off by Chukwu were usually sold as slaves.

Formally they were commonly sent by canoe, by a little creek to Old Calabar and disposed of there. If, however, the omen be pronounced to be favorable, the pilgrim is permitted to draw near to the shrine, and after various rites have been performed, the question is propounded, through the priests, and by them also, the reply is given. The votary (devotee) is given "Edo" (yellow powder) to rob around his eyes. He is also issued "Ofor-Chukwu"(little wooden carved images) as token of a person having actually consulted the sacred oracle. These "Ofor-Chukwu" are afterwards kept as dju-dju. A person who has been at Aro oracle after returning to his home, is reckoned dju-dju or sacred for seven days, during which period he must stay in his house, and people dreaded to approach him. He is a feared medicine man.

CHAPTER THIRTY-TWO

TELLING TIME

The periodic system by which time is measured in Igbo land is the same clock with long and short hands moving on a dial for twelve hours at a time, with indications of seconds, minutes and hours. The twenty-four hour day type system is used throughout Iboland, but in the absence of clock one can always approximate time by simply stepping outside and watching the position of the sun.

When the sun is directly overhead, we say it is noon anywhere in Igbo land. If the sun is slightly past over head, you know it is afternoon, and it is easy to be correct to the approximate minutes due to practice. The length of the shadow is another system the Ibos used to approximately tell time before the use of clock. The Ibos were closer to nature, relied on nature and were in working harmony with nature thousands of years before any professed naturalist or environmentalist. The land, the water, the air, the heavenly bodies, the animals all were counted as blessings, un-abused, cherished, consulted and nourished for the general good.

The sight of children coming home from school, the pre-schools and the primary pupils differentiating the times of the noon hours and the times thereafter. The palm-wine tappers use these customary occurrences to be on top of their trade in the triple threat of palm wine supply.

The sun rises at 6 am and sets at 6 pm throughout the year in Igbo land. At dawn, the cock (rooster) crows to signal or indicate day break. The first crow of the cock is heard at exactly 4 o'clock in the early morning. The second interval takes place at 5 o'clock, while the third is heard at 6'oclock am in the morning. If for any reason a cock miscalculates and crows at odd time in the night, the men will rise in the immediate family, find the cock and kill it., roast it and share the meat before going back to sleep. It was observed that mostly it is the first crowing cocks or roosters that miscalculate especially during full moon when the night is as bright as broad daylight. The rooster still meets its doom regardless.

ENGLISH	IGBO
Time	Oge
Clock	Igwe n'akowa oge
Hour	Elekere
Minute	Nkeji
Morning	Ututu
Afternoon	Ehihe uukori
Night	Uchichi ujishi
Evening	mgbede; uhuda, uhu
Early Morning	Isi ututu
Day	Ubochi
Clock is also called	"elekere"
Time may also imply	elekere

VALUE SYSTEM

Value in Igbo culture is seen in terms of having desirable or esteemed characteristics or qualities. Unfortunately, this is Webster's dictionary definition of valuable. The Ibo places less emphasis on the numerical quantity that is assigned or is determined by calculation or measurement. Then again, the later is one way Webster's dictionary defines value, hence the disparity in value systems.

Ibos have different value system than the Europeans. Relationship and family tradition heritage, village and the town's good name respectively, mean more to an Ibo man than great revenues.

The "dog eat monkey" and "cut throat" competition of today, that burning desire to conquer and amass wealth and material things, corrupt practices and greed were inherited from the Europeans, and readings on the Robber Baron, the Carnegies and the Standard Oil of California pioneers.

VALUED REFERENCES

IGBO CULTURE	EURO-AMERICAN CULTURE
PERSONAL	
Harmony	Excitement
Generosity	Thrifty
Obedience	Domination
Passive	Aggressive
Patience	Impatience
Wisdom	Knowledge
SOCIAL	
Cooperative	Competition
Sharing	Saving
Community	Individuality
Interdependence	Independence

FAMILY

(EXTENDED FAMILY)	(NUCLEAR FAMILY)
Respect for Children	Respect for Immediate Family
Respect for Parents	Family Security
Respect for Elders	
Respect for Relatives	

RELIGION

Chukwu	God
Chi	Jesus
Ofo	Holy Spirit

PHILOSOPHIC BASE

Humans in Cyclical Relationship with Nature	Human In Linear Relationship with Nature.
Man's Respect for Nature	Man in Control of Nature
Progress By Shared Responsibility	Progress by Inevitable Conflict

WEIGHTS AND MEASURES

The common units of measurement in Igbo land were the British systems, which were later on changed to the metric system. Prior to that period, the palm of the hand, the two palms of the hand, a closed fist, the foot print, the length of the arm, an average man's step all were convenient methods of measures. For instance, a closed fist is a good size of a piece of meat, one full palm of raw rice grains was equivalent to one quarter cup of rice, while two open palms is a measure of a cup of rice. In the local markets the length of an average man's arm from the sternum on the chest to the tip of the fingers was equivalent to a yard, if you were buying cloth, fishing strings or ropes. The entire length of both out-stretched arms was a measure of one's height.

UNIT WEIGHT	METRIC EQUIVALENT
Inch, foot, yard, mile	
Oz (ounce), 31.103 grams	
lb (pound) 0.373 kilogram	
score (twenty)	
gross (12 dozen/144)	
cwt - hundred weight (112)	
Ton - 100 cubic feet	
or 2240 lbs. (pounds)	

CAPACITY		METRIC EQUIVALENT
Gallon gal.	4 quarts	3.785 liters
Quart qt.	2 pints	0.946 liter
Pint pt.	4 gills	473.176 milliliters
Fluid ounce	fl. oz	
(water, milk, medication)		29.573 milliliters
Liquid ounce		
(minerals like gold, silver, nickel)		
Bushel bu.		(2219 cubic inches)

LENGTH

Inch in.	.083 foot	2.54 centimeters
Foot ft.	12 inches	30.48 centimeters
Yard yd.	3 feet	0.9144 meter
Rod rd.	16.5 feet	5.029 meters
Mile mi.	5280 feet/	
	1760 yards/ 320 rods	1.609 kilometers

HOUSEHOLD VOLUME

GALLON	4 QUARTS
QUART	2 PINTS
QUART	32 OUNCES (OZ)
PINT	16 OUNCES
GLASS	8 OUNCES
OUNCE	30 MILLILITERS

WEIGHT

POUND	16 OUNCES
2.2 POUNDS	I KILOGRAM
INCH	2.5 CENTIMETERS

NUMERICALS

Otu	1	One
Abuo	2	Two
Ato	3	Three
Ano	4	Four
Ise	5	Five
Isii	6	Six
Asaa	7	Seven
Asato	8	Eight
Ito-olu / Iteghete	9	Nine
Iri	10	Ten
Iri na out (ten plus one)		eleven
Iri na abuo (ten plus two)		twelve

10	Ten
20	Oogu/ Iri abuo
30	Iri ato (thirty)
100 Nari	(one hundred)
Puku	(one thousand) makes more sense in terms of money interpretation)
1,000, 000 Nde	(one million)
1,000,000,000 Njeri	(one billion)

The art of counting in Igbo language is lost for some time now. Families do no longer sit around fire places roasting maize and pear. The taste of cracked-white ash-coated roasted pear of early summer days may have been forgotten. The warm feeling of open fire places and smoky kitchens in a typical household in Igbo land during early corn and maize season is difficult to explain to an Ibo teenager born in California. Roasting yams on open fire, the smell of palm oil, sitting out in the village square during moonlight nights, these were when time appeared to be standing still.

Today, few Ibos can tell the equivalence of one thousand dollars in Igbo interpretation. It was easy when cowries were used, when kindergarten children used sticks to learn to count, and sometimes counted with their fingers and toes. Every child now uses calculators to do the most basic Arithmetic manipulation, and very little thought is put on the process of arriving at solutions Foreigner to Igbo land need not worry about learning to count in Igbo because Ibos themselves do not know it or use it in any transaction anywhere. Ibos know how to count in Igbo numerals but to convert $790, 000.00, the listing price of my house in Northern California, it will be a struggle.

CHAPTER THIRTY-THREE

SIGNIFICANT/ HISTORICAL EVENTS

The Ibos are very uniquely distinct and proud people. They are accused of being tenacious in their belief, audacious in their venture, intense in their resistance and suicidal in their persistence. It is no wonder Ibos fought to secede from Nigeria in 1967, but were not allowed to do so.

The central issue of 1962 census was whether the north had a larger population than that of the tworegions of south combined. The census showed the southern population to be equal to the north, but the British official in charge submitted that southern figures were false. The censusfindings were never published instead, a second census was held, in 1963, this time under the personal supervision of the Prime minister. This second census showed the north to be inhabited by 29.8 millions, and the southern regions by 25.8 million, giving the north a comfortable majority over the south. The figures were passionately contested and were rejected by most southern politicians. From 1966-1970, Nigeria was in a civil war. The Easterners, majority of whom were Igbo speaking wanted to secede to form the nation of Biafra. Nigeria resisted and tried to extirpate the Ibos in particular. It was a major sacrifice for human right, and the issues that led to that civil war still remain unresolved today. The war stripped the Ibos of their rights and privileges, and defined them into a minority role forever as Nigerians.

OJUKWU, BIAFRA FLAG, COWON, NIGERIA FLAG
By Chido Nwangwu

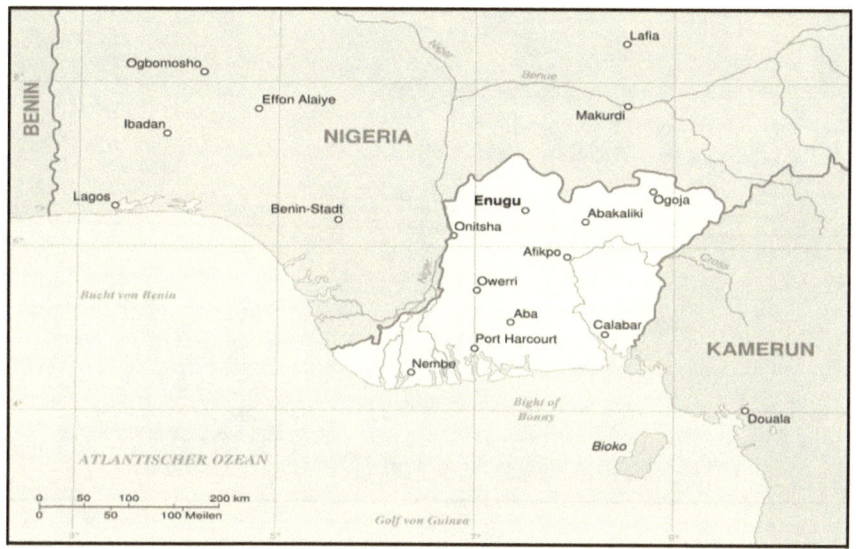

MAP OF THE STATE OF BIAFRA (1967-1970
(Source: Wikimedia Commons, the free media repository)

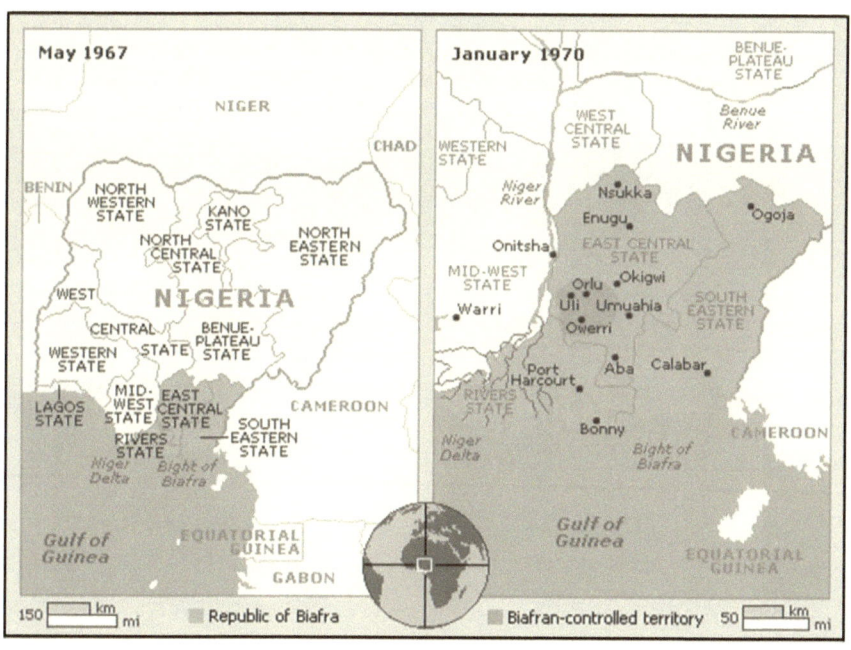

Before changing to Naira, the official currency of Nigeria was the British standard pound currency, shillings and pence. Part of Nigeria Independence was to do away with the British monetary system, hence the Naira and kobo.

BIBLIOGRAPHY

Chinue Achebe. A Man of the People. London, 1966; New York, 1966.

-------------------- No Longer At Ease. London, 1960; New York, 1961.

-------------------- Things Fall Apart. New York, 1959; London, 1958.

--------------------Things Fall Apart (New York: Anchor Books. 1994

Afigbo, A.E.   (1981)Ropes of Sand (Studies in Igbo History and Culture) Ibadan University Press, Ltd.

Bleeker, Sonia. The Igbo of Biafra. William Morrow and Company, New York,1969.

Bohannam, P. (1964) Africa and Africans. New York: The Natural History Press

Coursey, D.G. (1976) Yams. London : Green and Co.

Equiano, O. (1976) Equiano's Travels. Paul Edwards London: Heinemann Books Ltd.

CYPRAIN EKWENSI. People of the City. London, 1963.

Geertz, C. (19775) The Integration of Cultures. London: Hutchinson Publishers.

K.A.B.JONES-QUARTEY. A Life of Azikiwe. London, 1965; Baltimore, 1965.

JOHN HATCH. NIGERIA: The Seeds of Disaster. Chicago, 1970

Uchendu, Victor. The Igbo of Southeast Nigeria. New York: Holt, Rinehart and Winston, 1965

Chuku, Gloria. Igbo Women and Economic Transformation in Southeastern Nigeria.1900 – 1960.

New York: Routledge, 2005.

Korieh, Chima L…, and G. Ugo Nwokeji, eds. Religion, History and Politics in Nigeria. Lanham: University Press of America. 2005.

"Nigeria" The World Book Encyclopedia. Vol. 14. Chicago: world Book, 1986.

Noble, Judith et. al. The Hispanic Way: Aspects of Behavior, Attitudes and Customs in the Spanish-Speaking World, Lincolnwood, Chicago, Ill , NTC Publishing Company, 1992.

Nsugbe, Phillip O. Ohaffia: A Matrilineal Ibo People, Oxford: Clarendon Press. 1974.

Doumbia, Adama and Naomi. The Way of the Elders. Saint Paul, Minnesota: Llewellyn Publication, 2004

ABOUT THE AUTHOR

Columbus Onwujekwe Okoroike was born in Okai Village in Umuna Okigwe.

He grew up in Umuna Okigwe and Lagos Nigeria.

After his Secondary School Education, he joined Lever Brothers Nigeria Ltd, 15 Dockyard Road, Apapa, Lagos, Nigeria as Financial Accounting Clerk 1974 -1979

He attended Southern University, Baton Rouge, Louisiana, USA where he earned BSc. Business Administration and Economics December 1982

MA – Political Science and History –December 1985

He also holds an MBA degree (May 1987) Jackson State University, Jackson, Mississippi

He now lives in Sacramento, California with his wife and four children.

www.ingramcontent.com/pod-product-compliance
Lightning Source LLC
Chambersburg PA
CBHW022248290526
45785CB00015B/392